BEING

THE CRAFT OF MANAGING PEOPLE

THE

BOSS

L. KENT LINEBACK

BEING THE

THE CRAFT OF MANAGING PEOPLE

BOSS

Published under the sponsorship of the
IEEE Engineering Management Society

 IEEE
PRESS

The Institute of Electrical and Electronics Engineers, Inc., New York

Copyright © 1987 by
THE INSTITUTE OF ELECTRICAL AND ELECTRONICS ENGINEERS, INC.
345 East 47th Street, New York, NY 10017-2394
All rights reserved.

PRINTED IN THE UNITED STATES OF AMERICA

IEEE Order Number: PC02055

Library of Congress Cataloging-in-Publication Data

Lineback, L. Kent, 1943–
  Being the boss.

  ''Published under the sponsorship of the IEEE Engineering Management
Society.''
  Bibliography: p.
  Includes index.
  1. Personnel management. I. IEEE Engineering Management Soci-
ety. II. Title.
HF5549.L4945 1987   658.3   86-27751

ISBN 0-87942-212-2

Contents

. . . Moses sat to judge the people: and the people stood by Moses from the morning unto the evening . . .

And Moses' father-in-law said unto him, The thing that you do is not good. You will surely wear away, both you, and this people that is with you; for this thing is too heavy for you; you are not able to perform it yourself alone. Hearken now unto my voice, I will give you counsel . . .

*. . . **provide out of all the people able men** . . . **and place such over them, to be rulers of thousands, and rulers of hundreds, rulers of fifties, and rulers of tens:***

If you shall do this thing . . . then you shall be able to endure, and all this people shall also go to their place in peace.

EXODUS 17:13–24

Preface

This book grew from my own experience as a manager, particularly my experience helping develop new managers who worked for me. Based on that experience, I perceived a need for a clear, simple, action-oriented description of what managers, or bosses, really **do**—the fundamental activities required to manage people effectively.

You now hold the result of my perception in your hand. I hope you and other managers at many levels will find it helpful. If you are a new manager, it can help you learn on the job how to manage people. If you are an experienced manager, it can remind you of what is required to manage people effectively. And if you are a senior manager, it can serve as an aid in developing the skills of subordinate managers.

Let me be clear about my own point of view in this book. I do not doubt the value of management theory, but this book is not about theory. Nowhere does it define the manager's job as planning, staffing, directing and controlling. That description is not wrong; in fact, as a definition of the manager's functions, it is undoubtedly right. I just never found in my experience that it was very **helpful**. It never told me, the swamped manager, on a rainy Monday morning what I ought to do that day or that week. It did, on an occasional leisurely Friday afternoon, provide some guidance for the next month or the next year. Unfortunately, I found that such guidance too often dissolved in the flood of daily work.

So I wrote this book to be a manual for managers, a guide to action, an answer to the question, "What does the boss really do?" It is specifically about the management of people, the accomplishment of work through others, and not about the management of all resources, both human and non-human. To my mind, however, it is the management of people which affords the most excitement, satisfaction and frustration in management.

The excitement and satisfaction come from accomplishing something through others which you could not possibly do yourself. And the frustration comes from the sheer messiness of managing people. Seldom does anything turn out exactly as you hoped or expected; even if the results were satisfactory, you probably achieved them only after a ride through the white water of risk and uncertainty.

A small confession may be in order. I wrote this book because I am not a natural manager; the activities of managing people do not come easily to me. Thus I have always had to think carefully and deliberately about what I do as a manager. Major parts of this book, particularly Part III, were written over a period of years and are based on various problems I faced. Writing was a way for me to sort out my own thoughts, for I am one who usually does not know his own thoughts until they appear on a piece of paper. Writing has not made me a particularly good manager, but I think it has given me an awareness of what is basic to managing people. Do I always follow my own advice? Sometimes. But when I do not I usually find myself in trouble.

Being the boss is difficult, even when you know what you are supposed to do. It is an art, a craft, not a science or technology. So you must always remember that what I say here is little more than personal advice. It is a description of what I think works best for me. I have strong feelings about it, but what works for me may or may not work for you. Try it. Adapt it. Learn from it. Good luck.

How Is This Book Organized?

Some orientation and advice before you begin may help you get more from the book. It is roughly organized the way I think a manager's daily work organizes itself. The first priority is to get the work done. There are techniques for doing that, but problems inevitably arise and the manager must solve them. So, after an introductory section on the definition of management, this book follows that same scheme.

Part I—What Is Management?

What is management and why is it so difficult? This Part explores those questions and presents a basic strategy you can use in managing people.

Part II—Getting the Work Done

What does a manager do, if he or she doesn't "do" the work? The answer is the Fundamental Cycle of Management, a series of steps which the manager performs over and over again. They are what distinguishes the manager from every other professional.

Part III—Solving Problems

Solving problems ("putting out fires") is how most managers spend much of their time. This Part contains a series of short articles on the most common problems of management. Each article presents useful ideas and guidelines for action.

How Should You Use This Book?

You may do as you wish, but my advice is not to read the book cover to cover in one or two sittings. It is too densely written for that and contains too little entertainment; there is only one case and one or two short anecdotes. Instead, use it primarily as a reference manual. To do that effectively, however, you should:

1. Read Part I. There's a case history to spark it up, and it says some obvious things that are seldom said about the manager-subordinate relationship, which is the basis for everything else in management.

2. Work your way through Part II. Most of the sections within it are short and the way is clearly marked. In Part II you will have an opportunity to assess how well you already use the basics of managing people and to work out ways to improve your use of the basics. Read Chapter 5 ("What Is the Fundamental Cycle?"); evaluate your current use of the Cycle in Chapter 6; at the end of Chapter 6, after evaluating yourself, decide what actions you need to take, if any, to improve your use of the Cycle; then use Chapters 8–11 for help and guidance as you use the Cycle.

3. Part III is entirely reference material. Familiarize yourself with the chapter topics in it. Then, as problems arise, refer to the appropriate chapter.

Acknowledgments

More people than can be mentioned helped me write this book. Aileen Cavanagh of the IEEE provided valuable editorial suggestions and guided the manuscript through the approval process. Ray Keyes of Boston College and Ken Michel of GTE offered crucial encouragement when the book first began to take shape. Sterling Livingston, a former boss of mine, does not know yet that this book exists, but his hand is on it nonetheless.

PART I
WHAT IS MANAGEMENT?
(And Why Is It So Difficult?)

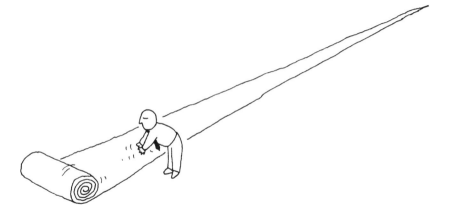

1 Introduction

The purpose of this book is to be a manual, a guide to action, but it must begin by looking at the setting within which that action occurs. Should you skip now to Parts II and III, and read them only, you would likely conclude that management is all technique—a series of steps, things to do. Technique is indeed important, even critical, but it exists to serve a purpose within a context. Describing that context is the purpose of Part I.

What follows are some conclusions I have drawn from my own experience. My intent is to convince you, if you need convincing, that the management of people is complex, difficult, and endlessly perplexing. It seems useful to me to explore briefly why that is so, if only to demonstrate the need for some of the steps and techniques which come later.

The best way to start is with a definition. While the practice of managing people is no less complex than the people themselves, the concept of management is straightforward:

A manager is responsible for accomplishing work through the efforts of others, rather than his or her own efforts as an individual worker.

Somehow the manager must accomplish the desired results by leading others. Management is thus a social activity, one that involves the interaction of two or more persons. At its very heart is the relationship between manager and subordinate. That relationship is the well from which accomplishment flows. If it is appropriately placed and properly constructed, it will produce copiously.

A short case history, a story, follows, for that is probably the easiest way to start talking about these things. The case does not prove anything. It simply gives us a common experience we can talk about. The case comes from the real experience of people I observed, but I have recast the location, names, and even the industry of those involved.

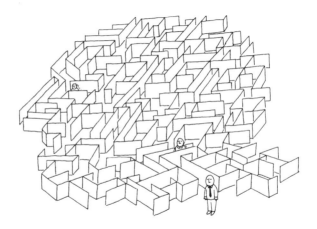

2 A Case: Bob Martin's Dilemma

AlphaBeta Systems Inc. specialized in developing computer software for businesses using mainframe and minicomputers. By 1982, the time of this case, it had grown to $30 million in sales. Most of the software it had developed and sold was for accounting purposes, such as payroll, accounts receivable, accounts payable, and general ledger. It typically used contract work to develop the background knowledge and experience with which to produce its own packaged software. The packaged software was then sold to other clients and was usually modified somewhat to meet each client's specific needs.

Bob Martin was Manager of Software Development. He had four systems analysts and six programmers working for him. Part-time programmers were also used as needed. Martin was a big, burly fellow, friendly, warm, and well over six feet tall, who had begun as a programmer. He had worked for several companies and had been a senior analyst with a client of AlphaBeta, when the Vice President of Software Development hired him for his current position.

As Software Development Manager, Martin was responsible for the development of all contract software, as well as major modifications to packaged software. Once a software package had been developed and was established in the market, it was taken over by the AlphaBeta marketing group, which sold it, handled all client contact, and made routine modifications in the software to meet client needs.

This position was Martin's first as a bona fide manager. In prior positions, he had served as project manager on a number of large-scale projects. It was that experience which made him attractive to AlphaBeta, in spite of his lack of management experience.

In fact, his coming had been a complete surprise to two system analysts who had wanted the position themselves. They learned of his coming on the day of his arrival. It had turned into a tense day. Martin had been perplexed about how to handle the resentment, though he knew it had not been directed at him personally. It was his natural warmth and lack of ego that ultimately reduced the tension. He had made clear he needed to learn his new job and had not come in to make sudden, sweeping changes. In fact, he went out of his way to spend considerable time with each of his subordinates, talking at length both about work and about personal topics. As a result of Martin's easy-going, friendly style, not only was there less tension, there was also better communication between members of his group. Before Martin's arrival, each project tended to be done as an isolated piece of work; after his arrival, there was much more mutual problem-solving and help.

Martin's dilemma involved the two analysts who had wanted his position—Jim Stanford and Terry Adams. Stanford had been with Alpha-Beta since almost its beginning in 1977. He had earned a reputation as an extremely bright and competent programmer and analyst. He had made major contributions to virtually every large project AlphaBeta had done. He too was a big fellow, with a heavy beard, and was known openly as Papa Bear. Around those he did not know well or respect, he was quiet and blunt when he had to speak. But with those he liked, he was warm and even paternal. It had taken several months, but his relationship with Martin had grown into one of real friendship. They had discovered their backgrounds were similar—both were physics majors in college. Both had been computer hackers and had built their own microcomputers in the late 1970's. They both loved to talk about computers, and about science fiction. Each had collected hundreds of science fiction books, and they kept up a running argument about which science fiction writer was the greatest of all.

Martin's relationship with Adams had also developed well, but had never extended beyond work. Adams was an electrical engineer who had worked his way through college largely through work as a programmer. In his late 20's, he had joined AlphaBeta only two years before but in that time had earned a reputation for tightly-run, well-managed projects that moved smoothly to completion, on time and in budget. Two or three clients had tried to hire him and he had almost left when Martin came. He also held an MBA degree with a heavy emphasis on data processing management. If anyone had pressed him he probably would have described computers as tools, perhaps more complex than most other tools, but still tools. That attitude was probably more bloodless than Stanford's or Martin's but it had no effect on the quality of his work or professional relationships. His relationship with Martin was warm but professional. They seldom talked about anything other than the work at hand, but he had mentioned once that he had stayed when Martin came because he felt he still could get broader experience at AlphaBeta.

After he had been at AlphaBeta almost a year, Bob Martin faced a decision which had him perplexed. Here's how he explained it at the time:

"We're very close now to landing a large development contract with one of our major clients. The work will be new for us because it will involve integrating microcomputers into a large company with a sophisticated data processing system. This client wants to tie all the micros into the mainframe system so they can either be used independently or as entry points into the mainframe processing system. There's a database system on the mainframe now. Our goal will be to revise and expand this system so it's accessible by the microcomputers. This kind of work is really exciting; I'm excited, we're all excited about it. It's the cutting edge. It's not just hardware and software—it's how organizations use data processing. Actually, it's more than that: it's how organizations use data, period. There will be major hardware and software problems, but I expect the organizational and policy issues will be just as tough. Who gets what access to what information? What can they do with it?

"Our plan is to do here what AlphaBeta has done in the past—develop a program or system for this client, then use the experience to develop a more generic program that we can sell to other clients. This client knows what we're going to do. They like it because it's a lever for them to negotiate the best price and they know it motivates us to do good work.

"This really is a major opportunity for AlphaBeta. This client is a very progressive company; in data processing, it's probably a year or two ahead of other companies. But the problem it wants to solve is going to be very common in the future. If we can develop a good software package now for integrating micros into a strong company-wide database system, we'll have a product to fuel our growth in the next few years. In fact, we hope this will help us double our sales in the next two or three years.

"My problem is choosing a system analyst who will have primary responsibility for the design of the system and the daily supervision of all programmers working on it. Because of experience and ability, my choice comes down to Jim Stanford and Terry Adams. Both of them want it and have told me they do. I have to make a final decision in a few days and I still don't know what to do.

"I wish there was some way that one of them was the obvious choice—so obvious that the other one agreed. Unfortunately, I think they're very close, though what each would bring to the project is different. They both are technically competent enough to do the job, but Stanford is probably the stronger of the two on the technical side.

On the other hand, Adams knows a bit more about database systems because of some of the work he did before coming here. And Adams probably knows more about the use of data processing in organizations because that's what he studied for his Master's degree.

"But when I come right down to it, I think the big difference between the two is really style, not substance. Stanford loves to sit down and noodle out a problem and talk about it—the theory, the ramifications, what it really means. Some people here, especially in marketing, think he's a little too blue-sky. Adams I think would rather spend his time worrying about how something is going to work. He tries to get to a reasonable solution real fast and then keep fixing it until it works. He'll choose a less elegant solution to a problem, if that is what it takes to get a solution. Stanford would have some trouble doing that. So if I put Stanford on the project, I could count on having the best possible, most elegant software. That may be just what's needed on this project. The software Adams produces wouldn't be so elegant, but it would certainly work.

"Both those guys are top people. I've worked with each really closely. You know they both wanted my job, so when I came, they weren't glad to see me. Especially Stanford. He's a little older and really wants to make a career move. I understand that. But now I think we work well together. I spent a lot of time talking to Stanford, and the others. We're a lot alike. I'm probably a little more polished than he is, and that's why I'm here. Anyway, it's not my style to look over people's shoulders, so I don't lean on him too much. I don't really have to. We usually end up talking at least every day or two. That's how I keep track. If he has any problem, it's his standards. They're real high, probably too high—for himself and everyone around him. He really puts programmers through a wringer. He's still the best programmer, even though it's not his job. But I don't see any more signs now of trouble with the programmers. One or two left–the weaker ones. Now that crew's pretty strong.

"Adams is first class, too. He doesn't open up as much as Stanford, but that's OK. They love him in Marketing because the clients like him. He was an MIS Manager in a little company once, so he understands where those guys are coming from. Stanford really presses those guys. Some of them aren't very good. A couple of times Marketing asked me to have Stanford back off some position with a client. Both times I think he was technically right. But I asked him to cool it because it was important to me, and he did. A month after I came here, I couldn't have done that. But now there's enough team spirit that I can. In fact I think we're getting the most out of all those guys that this company has ever gotten.

"If I had to choose one of them right now, which would it be? Probably Adams, I guess. There are other things involved in the work than just technical knowledge. The systems analyst on this project will have a lot of contact with the client, and I suppose Adams comes across better. He's probably a bit more flexible. I know Stanford has trouble putting up with fools. A lot of people fall into that category for him. For example, I have to laugh every time I think of this, but one time, Stanford attended a meeting with a client. The meeting was about some problems that had come up in a major modification Stanford was designing. Our marketing guy had an accident on the way and couldn't make it, so they had the meeting without him because it was mostly about technical stuff. Stanford told me about it a few days later when we were having a beer after work. Turns out Stanford and his counterpart with the client had some words. No big deal. This fellow had tried to suggest how to make some modifications in the software. The argument apparently ended when Stanford told the guy what he suggested was amateurish. He probably shouldn't have said that, but nothing really came of it, so I guess it turned out all right.

"I still have some trouble choosing one of them because this is really a team that's going to work on it—I'll be really involved and my boss (Vice President of Product Development) will be involved, too. I know Stanford could do an outstanding job. He and I work well together, and I think that maybe I could smooth over his rough spots. What makes it especially tough is that Adams would like the assignment, but Stanford wants it desperately. He thinks it's almost a career opportunity for him. If we eventually develop a generic product and it's big, there's the chance Stanford could transfer to Marketing and help manage the product there. I'm not too sure that's an opportunity for him, but he thinks it is. He is at a dead end at what he's doing now. Anyway, he's made it clear that he thinks he's better qualified for the project and should have it. I know Adams wants the project, too, but I'm not sure he feels as strongly about it as Stanford does."

3 Management Basics

Of course, this case is a cursory description of a complex problem; nonetheless, I believe the better choice for Martin was clear: assign the project to Adams. He had actual experience working with database systems, and the crucial aspect of this project was not only the data processing, but also the integration of the new system into the organization. In addition, Adams' personality and working style made him the obvious choice. This project required a great deal of interaction with client personnel. Because of his background and personal flexibility, Adams was the better choice. In addition, Adams' primary need was to make something work, while Stanford wanted to talk about theory. This apparently was not a fatal flaw for Stanford; I presume he had completed other projects successfully. Still, this new assignment would seem to have called for a master craftsman, not a theoretician.

Martin Failed To Do Four Basic Things

We need to focus on Martin, the manager. At first glance, he seems to have handled a difficult situation well as an outsider coming into AlphaBeta, and in many ways that impression is accurate. But he faced the dilemma in this case, I think, because he had simply failed to do some basic activities that all managers must do. As a result he was less effective than he could have been, for he was wavering over a decision that should not have been difficult to make. Let's look at those "basics."

FIRST, I believe **a manager must constantly evaluate the performance and**

abilities of subordinates. Only through working with and observing subordinates can you assess the strengths and weaknesses of each. That is necessary to make intelligent work assignments. From reading the case, we cannot tell whether Martin failed to evaluate Stanford thoroughly and frankly, or whether he simply refused to act on the results of his evaluation. In any case, he did not appear to be evaluating subordinates as he should have have been.

The SECOND "basic" is that I believe **a manager must constantly press for development and change** in the people who work for him, based on his evaluation of them. It was clear that Stanford had some major faults, particularly in relation to what he wanted to do—manage the design of this strategic project. Yet there was no evidence that Martin ever counselled him about those faults. When Stanford revealed that he had been too blunt with the client, Martin missed that opportunity to point out some better ways of handling such a situation. Nor is it clear that Martin ever talked to Stanford about his intolerance of those with less ability. We, of course, do not know how Stanford would have reacted to such a discussion. If he were to change, it would happen only if he wanted to change. He might have been totally blind to his own shortcomings. But that would have been a different problem. The primary problem was that Martin failed to press him to change—failed to help him change, failed to make clear that he needed to change, and was expected to change.

The THIRD "basic": I believe **every manager must constantly press subordinates to report on progress and evaluate themselves.** Martin never pressed Stanford to evaluate himself, to report on his own progress in various projects. He learned a revealing bit of information about a project while chatting over a beer. There was nothing wrong with that, but it makes me wonder about what Martin expected from his subordinates in reporting on their own work. I sense that Martin was hesitant to ask for progress reports— if necessary, to put his subordinates on the spot in a constructive way. I do not mean that a manager should go out of his or her way to create pressure on a subordinate. But the manager must make clear that subordinates must always be prepared to explain what is happening and why. Such reports are often the only way the manager can find out what is happening. Where progress can be measured in some objective way—e.g., sales, costs, time spent/lost, and so on—that is clearly preferable. Yet such objective information is not always available or appropriate, and when it is missing, the manager must ask subordinates to report on and evaluate their own work. Of course, this creates some pressure on the subordinates, even if it is done in a cordial and supportive spirit. There is some tension inherent in the act of asking, because you may be asking the subordinate to report bad news, almost to incriminate himself; you and the subordinate know that you must use any bad news in your continuous evaluation of performance. If a subordinate tells you he has completely mismanaged a task, that knowledge must affect your managerial opinion of him if you are to manage effectively. Martin's problem, I think, was that he preferred not to place any pressure on his subordinates; consequently, he seldom asked for real, candid, in-depth work assessments from subordinates, and that crippled his ability to assess their strengths and weaknesses, and to make intelligent work assignments.

The FOURTH "basic" was that Martin failed either to realize or to act on a hard fact of management life: **the requirements of work are more important than the individual desires of subordinates (and managers).** Stanford made clear to Martin that he wanted the assignment badly. It was important to him personally and professionally. That was also true of Adams, though I did not sense from what Martin said that Adams felt it was quite as crucial to his career. But to what extent should Martin strive to avoid disappointing Stanford? I believe that should have been a less important consideration. Only if all else had been equal should Martin have given great weight to Stanford's deeper desire for the assignment. Because all else was not equal, Adams should have received the assignment in spite of Stanford's strong personal need for it. Please don't misunderstand this. I am not saying that work is morally or philosophically more important than human beings and what they want or need—only that by the very nature of his work the manager must consider the requirements of work to have higher priority in the normal course of everyday events. Obviously, health and safety are more important, but once those needs are met, work must take priority. The individual needs and desires of employees (including those of the manager as an individual) may and should take precedence temporarily, and under special circumstances, but never for long.

The Wrong Relationship

I have a great deal of sympathy for Bob Martin. His problems remind me of those I have faced, particularly as a new manager. The heart of the matter, I think, was that he had gotten his relationships wrong with those who worked for him; at least, he had built an inappropriate relationship with Stanford. He had come into a difficult situation where key subordinates resented his presence. He had been successful in turning that resentment around, but he had done it essentially by saying, "I'm a decent fellow, just like you. I also share many of your values, likes, dislikes, and background." He built relationships on acceptance of himself, personally and individually, rather than as a professional, manager, and leader. He replaced the resentment with friendship, and it appeared he was motivating people by saying, in effect, "Do it because we're friends." I know from personal experience that such an approach can be very effective, but sooner or later it will create the kind of trap in which Martin finally found himself.

As a result, Martin was unable or unwilling to make the clearly appropriate decision. The reason seems clear: if he made that decision he would have destroyed the friendship he had built with Stanford. He did not appear to be friends to the same degree with Adams, so I suspect he felt his choice of Stanford would not have been as damaging to his relationship with Adams. Still, there was a good chance that whichever he chose, the other would probably leave; certainly, the loser would have been deeply disappointed. So Martin had created a problem for himself in which he would lose no matter which choice he made.

Can Manager and Subordinate Be Friends?

I believe this issue of friendship between manager and subordinate is a key one, worth exploring further. Let me say straightaway what I believe, hard as it may seem: A manager and subordinate cannot be true friends, for such a relationship will prevent the manager from being effective, and will inevitably lead to profound dissatisfaction for the subordinate. Let's look again at the various managerial activities Martin did not do.

Do friends evaluate each other? Martin apparently was not evaluating his subordinates continuously. Certainly, this was true of Stanford; even his weaknesses were described in favorable terms—"His standards are too high." Perhaps Martin was aware of Stanford's weaknesses, but if he was, he clearly did not weigh them sufficiently in his decision-making. As I said earlier, a manager must constantly evaluate, formally and informally, the abilities and performance of everyone who works for him. Such evaluation is necessary in order to accomplish the work through others. Yet I think it is equally clear that true friends do not evaluate each other in any significant way. Where they do evaluate, its purpose is to help the friend. Such help is also the primary reason for evaluations done by a manager. The difference is that in management, the evaluation is much more one-sided; and, in fact, the evaluation may lead to termination of the relationship. My conception of friendship is that whatever evaluation does occur will stop short of threatening the friendship itself. It is the nature of friendship that it persists in spite of shortcomings. It is the nature of the manager-subordinate relationship that it tries to remedy the weaknesses (of the subordinate, at least); but where the weaknesses are serious and indelible, they will end the relationship—a nice way of saying the subordinate will leave. Can you manage without evaluating subordinates? I believe the answer is an unequivocal "NO!" You would be foolish if you never think seriously about which subordinates can do which kind of work best. Yet I believe such evaluation is bound to strain the relationship between real friends.

Do friends press each other to change? It appeared that Martin was not pressing Stanford and Adams to change and grow professionally. Whatever Martin's decision was, he needed to have a long talk with Stanford about the various ways Stanford needed to change. We know from the case that Stanford needed to be more tactful and patient with others, and he probably needed to show more concern with the nuts and bolts of things. I have the feeling, though, that if Martin were to initiate such a discussion, it would have been their first. The case did not say that explicitly, but I feel confident in surmising it. Why? Because Martin and Stanford were good friends, and just as real friends generally do not evaluate each other seriously, neither do they seek seriously to change each other.

Unless everyone who works for you is perfect and completely adaptable, and unless the work never changes in any way, you will spend considerable time as a manager defining and re-defining the work and encouraging your subordinates to adapt, increase, or develop their skills. (By skills I mean all types of skills, social and managerial, as well as technical.) In short, you will constantly be trying to change the people who work for you. Development is change, and if you are developing people as a manager should, you will be urging change upon them constantly. The problem with change is that no one can force anyone else to truly change. All change and development is basically self-directed. You can force superficial and temporary change, but all real change comes from within the individual. To foster such real change, you must make the individual see the need for change. Yet every need to change is, by definition, a personal shortcoming; there is a difference between what the individual is, and what he or she should be. Every effort you make to foster change in an individual is an implicit criticism of that person. That, I believe, is why friends seldom try to change one another.

Of course, there are ways to help people see the need for change which are less irritating than others. It is possible to create situations where the individual involved will himself discover the need to change. Still, that is not always possible. Many times you, as manager, must state outright to subordinates that there is something either lacking or wrong with them which must change. That is a fact of management life, if the work is to get done in a changing environment. But we fool ourselves if we think it never leaves a bitter taste for the employee. It certainly is not the kind of behavior shown by friends to each other.

Do friends check up on each other? This issue is somewhat less straightforward, but again, we can approach it through the case. There is some irony here. One of the reasons Stanford may not win the assignment arose from a bit of information he himself provided to Martin. While chatting with Martin over a beer, Stanford revealed that he had called a client an "amateur" to his face. That gave Martin an insight into Stanford's personality that he should not have ignored as a manager. If and when Stanford discovered that he had lost the assignment, in part because of information he himself had provided, he would probably have felt betrayed because he had revealed that information socially to a friend.

Yet Martin obtained that information with a technique every manager must use—he asked a subordinate for a progress report. I believe such reports are absolutely necessary if a manager is to obtain necessary information. By "progress report," I do not mean the kind of simple "What's happening?" question that Martin apparently asked during casual conversations. "Progress report" for me refers to a series of "What,"

"Why," "When," "What if," and "What then" questions. The level of detail plumbed with these questions will depend on the subordinate's experience, the manager's confidence in the subordinate, and the risk involved in the work at hand. But I believe every manager at every level must ask those questions of subordinates in some way. Yet I suspect that Martin was not asking them, and the reason can be found again in the relationship between Martin and Stanford.

Progress reports present no problem if the work is going well. All of us love to pass on good news. But what if the work is not going well? How candid do you really expect the subordinate to be? In theory, you should expect complete candor, but in practice, that is probably unrealistic. You are asking the subordinate to report on himself; if the news is bad, you and he know that you must use that news to modify your professional opinion of him. Can you avoid asking for progress reports? Not if you want to be in control of events, and able to take corrective steps when there are problems.

But how does the subordinate feel about being asked, when he knows the information will be used to evaluate him? Based on my own experience as subordinate and manager, I suspect the subordinate's attitude is often one of slight resentment. The request for a progress report has an air of "checking up" by the manager, an implication of distrust—otherwise, why would the manager not wait until the work was done to see how it comes out? Many of us dislike the obvious implication that we might fail, and we resent the idea that we may not find some solution to the obstacles we face.

Given that, I believe it is clear why Martin apparently never pressed Stanford for progress reports. To press him would have threatened their relationship, which Martin probably believed was one that produced the best possible work from Stanford. Real friends don't really check up on each other in quite the same way as managers must seek information from subordinates; nor do friends use the information gained for evaluating each other in quite the same way.

Do friends consider work more important than each other? I said earlier that the manager must ultimately give highest priority to the accomplishment of the work for which he or she is responsible. Unfortunately, this means that the work is sometimes more important than the individual hopes and desires of all the individuals involved, including the manager. It is the manager's job to implement that hierarchy of values, even upon himself. But how do you tell a friend that something is more important than the friend, particularly something as impersonal and mundane as a job assignment for which the friend feels clearly qualified? In his own mind, Stanford was simply saying, "Give me what I deserve anyway, that's all I want." Of course, we can say hard things to friends. But there is always the risk saying them will destroy the friendship, so I suspect we usually keep quiet.

In the end, Martin faced his dilemma because of his own shortcomings as a manager. He essentially built the wrong relationship with subordinates.

With at least some of them, it was a relationship of friendship. And friendship, for all the reasons just cited, is fundamentally incompatible with the requirements of management.

The Manager-Subordinate Relationship Is Unique

How did Bob Martin create this trap for himself? How did he come to develop the kind of relationship that was reducing his effectiveness? I suspect it simply happened, as it did with me as a new manager, and as I have seen it happen with others. In fact, I suspect it happens quite a lot, for all the reasons that follow.

I believe the relationship between manager and subordinate, in its proper form, is unique in our culture. There is no other quite like it. Unfortunately, I do not believe that is said clearly and compellingly enough to managers, particularly new managers. Thrown into the water to swim on his own, the new manager will build his relationship with subordinates in whatever way he feels appropriate. Most likely, he will choose as a model some other relationship with which he is familiar. There are several to draw from: parent-child, teacher-pupil, manipulator-pawn, friend-friend, and probably many more not worth listing here. None is entirely appropriate as a model, though each has features which may make it seem appropriate. Martin seemed to choose the friend-friend model; that is, he consciously or unconsciously chose to be friends with those who worked for him, and for whose work he was responsible.

The problem created by such a relationship in a management context is that the subordinate-friend will ultimately feel betrayed, his expectations of his manager-friend disappointed in some way. The other relationships mentioned above are little better, but for different, and mostly obvious reasons. The difficulty is that we usually fail to recognize that we are creating a relationship in the image of another, different relationship. Often, we take bits from one relationship and pieces from another, as may the subordinate. The subordinate may be modeling his or her part of the relationship after a different model. Of course, the model used by either manager or subordinate is what determines the unspoken expectations held by each; and the expectations are what can prepare the way for disappointment, disillusionment, and demotivation.

The difficulty I've found with the manager-subordinate relationship is that, like most other human relationships, it is not only unique, but also immensely complex. The lucky new manager is one who has worked for a good manager—that is, a manager who did create the appropriate relationship. The new manager can use that experience as a model. Without that experience, another new manager must somehow find the appropriate relationship by trial and error. My sense is that many managers never quite discover it, and many, many more intuitively know what it is, but do not quite understand how to carry it out in daily practice.

The Paradox of Management

The root of the difficulty in building the proper manager-subordinate relationship is that the relationship contains a fundamental paradox. Having read this far, you might have concluded that the relationship ought to be distant, cool, and formal—what lawyers call an "arms-length" relationship. While I understand how you might have reached that conclusion, I believe it is totally wrong; and that is why I say the manager-subordinate relationship is a paradox.

It Cannot Be a Relationship of Real Friends...

I hope I have convinced you that for the reasons already given, the manager-subordinate relationship cannot be one of true friendship. If it is, it will ultimately impair the effectiveness of the manager and the motivation of the subordinate. Yet I deeply believe the relationship ought to be a friendly, warm, and cordial one. That is, it ought to be a natural one—one that reflects the human natures of the people involved. If those involved are not particularly warm and open people, the relationship will not be either— nor should it be. If they are, the relationship ought to reflect that, too, and it can, without creating a relationship of true friendship, but only if friendship is consciously avoided. For example, I personally have found it unwise to socialize a great deal with subordinates away from work; nor do I particularly want to socialize a great deal with my boss. I also think it would be unwise for my wife to become close with the wife of a subordinate, or the wife of my boss. Those things do happen, and people survive, but I have found they create the potential for problems by creating the wrong expectations. Yet, I hope my relationships with boss and subordinates are open, caring, graced with some laughter, cordial—in other words, friendly. But in no way should those relationships become ones of true friendship, for friendship is a tie between two people that exists for itself, that fills some deep human need in each of us, and that will seek to perpetuate itself in spite of problems and shortcomings. That is very different from the manager-subordinate relationship, which exists only to perform specified work.

Nor Can It Be a Cold or Distant Relationship...

The second side of the paradox is that the manager cannot allow the relationship to be distant or filled with discord. The reasons for this have nothing to do with what is socially "nice," but with the need to accomplish work. Where the relationship is one of dislike or discord, the manager is less likely to see, and use appropriately, the subordinate's strengths. The manager must always be able to see a subordinate clearly and fairly, and must allow that subordinate to develop and change. Where the relationship is too formal or distant, the manager will have difficulty helping the subordinate see the need for any change. And where the relationship is less than warm, the subordinate will probably be less willing to provide candid and complete information about work to the manager.

To get the best from subordinates, to motivate them, the manager must know and understand them as individuals. What does each like? Dislike? What skills does each possess, small as well as large? When is each up? Down? What are the personal quirks of each? When does each shine? What motivates each one? What in the personal life of each is relevant to his or her work? All this knowledge is needed for the manager to make intelligent judgments about what assignments and overall responsibility to give (or not to give) a subordinate. To make these kinds of judgments, the manager must know subordinates almost as well as friends know each other. To know people this well requires that the manager spend time with them, talking about a wide variety of subjects. In other words, the manager must be close to subordinates. And to obtain their commitment to the work and the manager's leadership, the manager must treat them with respect and humanity.

Now you see why I say the manager-subordinate relationship is a paradox. It is not one of true friendship, but it should be close. It should be warm, friendly, and respectful on both sides—but always based on the clear understanding that it exists to accomplish the work.

Summing Up

My goal in this chapter has been to convey some sense of the complexity, ambiguity, and apparent contradictions with which managing people is filled. I wish that the management of people could be reduced to some simple concepts, a four-cell matrix that captures its essence. But it cannot be, and anyone who says it can is misleading you. All the accomplishments of a manager spring from the manager's relationship with subordinates. That relationship is unique and cannot be based on any other relationship, particularly not the relationship that exists between true friends. Yet the relationship between manager and subordinate must be warm, close, and cordial. No wonder managing people is so difficult.

The rest of this book is about exactly that—managing people effectively in the face of that difficulty. There is no magic answer, no secret, just a strategy and a technique for carrying out that strategy.

But before going on, let me impart the one piece of advice you would need if you were to read nothing more of this book, or any other book on management: hire the absolute best people you can. If you can find someone better than you, hire that person right away. Of course, you must motivate good people, and good people will stretch your own capabilities as manager and professional. But those challenges will be trivial compared with the problems caused by mediocrity and incompetence. Having good people will compensate for many of your own weaknesses and will require a relative minimum of supervision. No strategy, no technique, can entirely correct the problems caused by poor choice of people.

4 A Strategy for Managing People

This chapter presents a strategy for building and maintaining the kind of relationship with subordinates that will best foster the accomplishment of work. It is not a panacea for the complex problems of managing people. Rather, I hope it will serve as a rough and ready guide.

I believe that in managing people, the manager's strategy ought to be:

ALWAYS FOCUS ON THE WORK AND NOTHING ELSE.

That may strike you as somewhat obvious. After all, it is the manager's job to accomplish the work through others. But I am speaking here about practice, not principle. The principle is obvious; putting it into practice is difficult. You manage a group of people. There is prescribed work to be done by this group. Yet, day after day, you find yourself pulled away from the work by hundreds of problems (most of them ultimately trivial). It is difficult, though it sounds easy, to keep your attention on the purpose of it all—the work: getting it done, in budget, and up to quality standards.

In order to guide action, this strategy must be more specific, so I have reduced it to four fundamental guidelines:

Focusing Fundamental #1: Strive to clarify the work—make sure it is well defined, including the objectives and the roles of the people doing the work.

If the objectives of those under you are not clear, and if the individual role of each person is not clear, then the work is not likely to be done satisfactorily. The reasons are obvious: if people do not know what they are supposed to do, they probably will not do what they should. A less obvious reason, but an equally compelling one: where people are not clear about what they should be doing, they tend not to take personal responsibility for their work. Clarity and the willingness to take responsibility are intimately related; it is difficult to have the second without the first. I believe real motivation requires that sense of personal responsibility.

Defining responsibility for work is a complex, never-ending management task. I often find myself hoping it can be done once and forever. In fact, it is never finished, because the world never stops changing, and our understanding of it constantly grows. What changes, in particular, is how the abstract definition of someone's responsibilities applies to the messy, concrete details of everyday work. That is where most of your "defining" will be required.

Understand: Defining work is more than a simple matter of telling a subordinate, "All right, here's what you do. Now do it." It should include setting the context of the work—why it must be done, how it fits in the larger scheme of the organization, who will use the product of the work and what they need, and so on. Defining work means conveying to people the significance of what they are responsible for. Without that significance, work can hardly have any meaning or provide any satisfaction.

In the Bob Martin case, whoever is chosen for the new assignment, Martin must explain to him as precisely as possible what is required, what will constitute acceptable and unacceptable work, and the importance of the project (its context) for the company as a whole. If Martin had done that kind of defining earlier with Stanford, then Stanford might have discovered his own shortcomings, and even corrected them sufficiently to merit the assignment he wanted.

Focusing Fundamental #2: Build all your relationships with subordinates around the work.

Before you became a manager your relationships with people at work were probably built on a variety of foundations: common interests, shared work, similar goals, related backgrounds, compatible social instincts, and so on. But I believe there can be only one basis for your relationship as a manager with those who work for you: the work that must be done. That is the center of your role as a manager. It is the anchor of your authority. Everything you do must ultimately come back to it in some way.

Martin's problem in the sample case was that he had failed to focus the relationship with Stanford on the work alone. He then faced a difficult problem in that he and Stanford had become friends. At that point, there was no easy solution. But Martin somehow had to find a way to focus the relationship on the work, if he wished to be fully effective.

If you feel that such a relationship is very limited, my answer is yes, it is, but that is exactly the point. Every time you build the relationship on something other than work, you will diminish your ability to get the work done through people. If you say that such a relationship sounds dull, my answer is that it need not be. A relationship built around a common work goal can be extremely cordial, engrossing and deeply, humanly interesting. But you must make clear that the relationship exists in order to accomplish the work. If your primary goal is to form warm, close relationships with other people, you probably should not be a manager.

If you do not center your relationships with subordinates around the work, you will then have great difficulty giving highest priority to the work itself, and you will have difficulty objectively evaluating your subordinates' abilities to do various aspects of the work. In short, you will diminish your effectiveness as a manager. If you do not believe the work you do is worth that kind of commitment, I believe you should think about changing your work.

Perhaps you are thinking, "But I manage people, not robots!" Nothing here implies that people should ever be treated as less than full human beings. You are engaged with those who work for you in the pursuit of a common goal—the successful completion of the work, whatever it is. For purposes of getting the work done, you have been given a position of authority over these people. This does not mean that you are in any way better than they. Your position of authority only applies to the work at hand. If you try to extend your position beyond that narrow focus, you will complicate the relationship and invite trouble.

It may help to keep this distinction in mind: Focus on the work done by people, not on the people doing the work.

Focusing Fundamental #3: Use the work itself to develop and motivate the people doing the work.

I find it useful to think this way about what a manager does: A manager accomplishes work by developing the abilities of subordinates and then motivating those subordinates to apply those abilities effectively to accomplish the work.

The problem is that we tend to separate the tasks of motivating and developing from the actual "doing" of the work. When the pressure is on, we tend to say, "Tomorrow we can motivate and develop people. Today this shipment has to get out." Yet, in this case, management is like the rest of life—tomorrow never comes.

This is a serious problem that will always exist so long as we think of motivation and development as separate from the daily work. In fact, I believe they should be inseparable from the daily work. The trick is to use the daily work to motivate and develop people. Define, assign, and follow-up that work in such a way that when it is done, the subordinates involved will be more able and willing than before. Doing this requires that you approach your work with a certain attitude or point of view. That is, each time a task or problem arises, you must ask yourself, "How can we handle this in a way that will help develop or motivate someone?"

Martin, for example, might have assigned another, less crucial project to Stanford which required a non-theoretical approach and heavy client contact. Then, Martin could have worked closely with Stanford to develop and apply those skills which he lacked in sufficient measure. But without asking himself, "How can I use this work (the less crucial project) to make someone better?", Martin would have assigned that work to an analyst who already possessed in full such skills. The project in the case was far too important to use for this purpose.

Focusing Fundamental #4: Manage systematically.

At one time I worked for a man, an astute professor, who had spent much time studying the practices of effective managers. He once commented to me that every good manager he knew was systematic; the good manager, he said, figured out what needed to be done and he or she set up a system for conscientiously getting it done. Thus, I believe the successful application of these Focusing Fundamentals requires a system—that is, a series of related steps faithfully followed.

By "system" I do not mean a rigid series of activities which allow no flexibility. Instead, "system" here refers to a framework of actions which allow flexibility but insure that the essential activities of management get done in a way that focuses on the work. Such a system also contributes to clarity, for it helps make known to all concerned what the manager expects.

In fact, the system is a cycle—a series of basic steps which are repeated over and over. I call it the Fundamental Cycle of Management. It is the subject of the next Part, and it is the heart of this book.

Summing Up

In managing people, focus on the work to be done. . .

- Always make sure the work is clearly defined.
- Build your relationships with subordinates around the work and nothing else.
- Define, assign, and follow-up the daily work so it is done in a way that motivates and develops the people doing the work. (Real development of people cannot occur off-line.)
- Use a system for managing to make sure the right management activities get done at the right times.

PART II
GETTING THE WORK DONE
(The Fundamental Cycle of Management)

5 What Is the Fundamental Cycle of Management?

When I first became a manager I remember wondering how to answer that question which often appears on questionnaires: "What is your occupation?" I was a manager, but to write "manager" did not seem specific enough. Would they know what it meant? Did I know what it meant? It seemed to me that other occupations were clearly characterized by certain specific and unique activities: baseball players played baseball. Doctors diagnosed and treated patients' ailments. Architects designed buildings. Engineers made or built things. Lawyers kept each other busy. But what did managers do that set management apart from other occupations?

The key, I finally decided, was that most behavior which characterized various occupations was repetitious—it was done over and over, whatever "it" was. So I looked in my own work for what I did (or perhaps should have been doing) over and over. I realized then that there is indeed a set of activities which are the essence of managing people and which managers repeat over and over. I came to think of this set of activities as the Fundamental Cycle of Management. It is composed of the following steps.

The Fundamental Cycle of Management

Step 1: The manager reviews the basic purpose of the work unit for which he or she is responsible. What is the reason for its existence? What is it really trying to do?

Step 2: The manager then sets a direction for the work unit as a whole and makes sure there are specific, reasonable targets or standards identified for pursuit during a specified time into the future.

Step 3: The manager provides leadership to make sure that the work unit accomplishes the work targets set in Step 2. This is the longest, most important step, for it is here that the work is actually accomplished.

Step 4: Once the work specified in Step 2 has been accomplished (or not), the manager leads the work unit through a review of the experience in order to learn from it.

These steps are carried out over the course of a period, then are repeated during the following period and every period after that. Thus, it is a cycle.

A period is a specified length of time, as selected by the manager (or by the organization for which the manager works). The usual period for accounting purposes is one year, with the year broken into quarters of three months each. A period for the Cycle can be anywhere from one week to one year long, depending on the demands of the work and how rapidly the work environment changes. A week is probably too short; everyone involved will be spending all their time planning instead of doing, and little will get done. A year is probably too long; there will not be enough reviewing and learning from experience. I have found that a period of one quarter is about the right length of time for repeating the steps of the Fundamental Cycle. (It also integrates nicely with the annual/quarterly accounting cycle most organizations use.)

Understand that the Cycle is a process, a sequence of steps. The sequence is the same for each period, but the content of each step is different. For example, each period the manager sets targets for accomplishment in that period. The act of setting targets is the same for each period, but the specific targets to be accomplished will be different. Thus, the process is always the same, but the content of the process is always different.

I'm sure that none of the above steps is new to you. Certainly, this manual is not the first time they have ever been identified. Yet, obvious as they may seem, try to think of how many managers you know who consistently follow them. Again: the concept is simple; the activity is difficult. I have found, for example, that the Cycle is a fairly natural set of activities; that is, each part flows logically from the previous and into the following. Each part "feels" like the appropriate thing to do at the time. Nonetheless, it is always easier not to do the steps, because of the pressure of time and events. As a manager, you will have to require the completion of each step. Otherwise, they will not be done consistently.

Unfortunately, the mere following of the steps in the Cycle will not guarantee success. You can fail, for example, because you did not set and singlemindedly pursue targets. Or you can fail because you set and pursued the wrong targets. The Cycle and this manual deal necessarily with the first problem only; if you follow the steps outlined here you will certainly set targets. Setting the **right** targets is up to you.

Step 1: Review Your Basic Purpose

Purpose: To review what you and your work unit are responsible for and how your performance will be evaluated; also, to make sure your unit is organized appropriately for those responsibilities.

Basic Elements: However you carry out this Step, it should include:

1. A clear definition, in writing if possible, of what you (your work unit as a whole) are responsible for.

2. A clear definition of how your performance will be evaluated; what will constitute good, adequate, and unsatisfactory performance.

3. A clear definition of how your work unit is organized—who is responsible for what and how performance will be evaluated in each case under those responsibilities.

4. A quick but thoughtful review of your work unit:

- Is it organized properly to get the work done well?
- Is there a good matchup between jobs and people?
- Does each subordinate reporting directly to you understand what he or she is responsible for?
- Are the resources provided/available to your work unit sufficient in general for it to accomplish its purpose?

5. An awareness and acceptance of the above by your boss and direct subordinates.

Step 2: Set a Direction

Purpose: To identify the specific accomplishments you and your work unit will achieve in the next period.

Basic Elements: However you carry out this Step, it should include:

1. Overall direction and performance targets/standards set by you for your work unit for the next period, with the input and knowledge of your boss.

2. Specific performance targets/standards established for each subordinate reporting directly to you.

3. Where appropriate, action plans and budgets (i.e., a clear definition of the resources needed) for achieving the targets set by each subordinate reporting to you.

4. Communication of your unit's plans to others in the organization who need to know.

Step 3: Provide Leadership

Purpose: To lead your work unit so it can successfully implement the plans, and achieve the targets, set in Step 2.

Basic Elements: However you carry out this Step, it should include:

1. A calendar set up by you showing all the key checkpoints and deadlines for your work unit for accomplishing the targets.

2. Identification and development (during the period) of the information and analysis needed to track progress against the targets.

3. Regular meetings and systematic communications between you and your direct subordinates to review progress (i.e., to review the calendar, information, analysis and so on).

4. Some method for revising plans or re-allocating resources when appropriate.

5. Periodic progress reports to your boss and others in the organization who need to know.

Step 4: Learn from Experience

Purpose: To learn and improve by reviewing what was and was not accomplished during the last period.

Basic Elements: However you carry out this Step, it should include:

1. A self-appraisal by each direct subordinate of his or her performance during the period.

2. An appraisal by you of your work unit's overall performance, including your performance as manager.

3. An appraisal by you of each subordinate's performance, followed by a meeting with each subordinate to discuss ways the subordinate can improve performance.

4. A review with your boss of your unit's performance, and your performance as manager.

Some Further Comments on the Cycle

Notice that the Cycle is based on a model of how people learn. Its purpose is to accomplish the work, but to do so in a way that develops those doing the work. The Cycle itself is a good example of the learning model presented in Chapter 13 (''Helping Subordinates Learn'').

The Cycle is a good way to make clear what you expect of people in their work. Clarity is a theme that weaves through this manual. I believe people are reluctant to take personal responsibility for results unless what is expected of them is clear—what should be done, when, and at what standard of quality. Of course clarity alone is not sufficient; inadequate resources, for example, can create failure too. Still, I think clarity is the first requirement. A personal sense of responsibility is crucial to motivation, for where the work is ambiguous, people will be reluctant to take responsibility. The Cycle is a basic way of providing clarity.

The Cycle allows great flexibility in management style. You can carry out the Cycle with or without significant participation by subordinates. For example, you may set targets for each subordinate, or allow subordinates to suggest their own targets. The Cycle itself is silent on the question of which is better; it only demands that reasonable targets of some kind be set under your overall leadership. My intent here is not to avoid an important issue (whether to allow subordinate participation or not) but to observe the proper priorities. To worry about how something is done—the question of style—before understanding what needs to be done seems to me inappropriate. It is as if an actor worried about how to say his lines before he memorized them. Work on doing the right things, and then worry about style—that is, the details of how to do them.

Your boss is important in the Cycle. You need his or her support, for example, to obtain the help and resources required. However, your boss can be involved only as much as he/she wants to be. You will have to assess that level of interest and work with it. Involve your subordinates too, as you feel appropriate. You depend on them, for in most organizations you will rise or fall on their shoulders. In general, get all the help, support, and information you can, from your boss, your subordinates and your peers.

There is no reason that the process involved in the Cycle cannot be known by everyone involved. I believe it should be an open process, visible to all. (Of course, the content of the Cycle—e.g., specific targets set—may be confidential.) Indeed, the process ought to be so natural and obvious that it is virtually invisible, or at least unremarkable.

Do not feel that following the Cycle will stifle your creativity or ability to respond innovatively to challenges or change. Following the Cycle will, I think, increase your creativity once you have become accustomed to it, because it will free you from having to worry about the simple basics. (What are we trying to do? Are we really doing it?) You will know that these basics are, and will be, taken care of. I cannot emphasize this point too strongly: Followed intelligently and flexibly, the Cycle will give you the freedom to be creative.

One final but extremely important comment: Do not be deceived by the apparent simplicity of the Cycle. It looks very neat on paper, but in actual use it is messy. I have found that it never comes out quite the way you planned or hoped. Something is always missing or different from what you thought it would be. To carry it out, simple as it seems, is incredibly hard work.

The next chapter, beginning on the following page, is a series of questions that will help you assess how well you are now following the Cycle in your work as a manager. You should proceed to those questions next.

Chapters 7 through 11 concern the use of the Cycle in your work. They provide a detailed set of actions for carrying out each Step in the Cycle, along with "Detailed Notes" on each action.

6 How Well Are You Using the Fundamental Cycle?

In this section you will have an opportunity to look at how well you now use the Fundamental Cycle. The Cycle is presented here as a series of questions paralleling the key elements of each Step in the Cycle as outlined in the previous section.

Work through the questions. For every question the correct answer is a definite Yes. Answers such as No, Sometimes, Maybe, or Yes, but . . . indicate a need for improvement. The questions are designed to be answered quickly. Candor, rather than deep thought, is more helpful here.

Following the questions is a section in which you can note any plans for improvement. The Detailed Notes will help you with more information and advice about specific parts of each Step.

Step 1: Review Your Basic Purpose

Purpose: To define what you and your work unit are responsible for and how your performance will be evaluated; also, to make sure your unit is organized appropriately for those responsibilities.

Key Questions:

1. Do you clearly understand what you and your work unit are responsible for?

2. Do you clearly understand how your performance will be evaluated?

3. If you ask your boss, would he/she give the same answers to the above questions as you?

4. Are the responsibilities of your direct subordinates clear in your mind?

5. Are the responsibilities of your direct subordinates clear in their minds?

And is their understanding essentially the same as yours? (How do you know?)

6. Are you and each of your subordinates in agreement about how his/her performance will be evaluated?

7. Is your work unit as a whole generally adequate for its purpose? Does it possess the overall skills and resources required? If not, you must go back to the beginning and rethink your purposes, or find additional resources.

8. Is your work unit organized effectively? That is:

- Are the right people in the right jobs?
- Does each position report to the most appropriate position?

Review your answers and note any opportunities for improvement.

Step 2: Set A Direction

Purpose: To identify the specific accomplishments you and your work unit will achieve in the next period.

Key Questions:

1. Do you operate now based on some definite regular planning period–a year, half-year, quarter or month? If so, what is it?

2. At the beginning of each period, do you work out a general direction and set some overall targets or standards (with your boss's agreement) for your work unit?

3. Do you communicate those overall directions/targets/standards to your immediate subordinates and ask them to work out related targets in their individual areas of responsibility?

4. Do you review specific action plans and budgets developed by your subordinates for their targets, whenever that is appropriate? Do you consistently make sure that adequate resources are available for implementing the plans?

5. Are others in your organization who need to know your plans adequately aware of them?

Review your answers and note any opportunities for improvement.

Step 3: Provide Leadership

Purpose: To lead your work unit so it can successfully implement the plans, and achieve the targets, set in Step 2.

Key Questions:

1. Do you systematically keep track of key checkpoints and deadlines for each of your direct subordinate's targets?

2. Have you and your subordinates identified the basic information and analysis needed to keep track of progress toward each target?

3. Do you meet regularly with each subordinate to discuss progress toward targets?

4. Do you strive to make your unit's plans work, and are you willing to revise plans or reallocate resources when necessary?

5. Do you report periodically and regularly to your boss on your unit's progress?

Review your answers and note any opportunities for improvement.

Step 4: Learn From Experience

Purpose: To learn and improve by reviewing what was and was not accomplished during the period, and why.

Key Questions:

1. At the end of each period, do you review your unit's overall performance (and your own as manager) and write a formal report?

2. Do you ask each subordinate to appraise in writing his or her own performance at the end of each period?

3. Do you appraise each subordinate in writing and then meet with them to review your appraisal and compare it with the subordinate's self-appraisal? Is the purpose of these meetings to find ways your subordinates can improve their performance?

4. Do you review your unit's performance with your boss?

5. Do you use what was learned during each period to improve your unit's performance in succeeding periods?

Review your answers and note any opportunities for improvement.

A Self-Development Plan

Review all the opportunities for your own improvement which you identified on the previous pages. Note the most important ones that you plan to pursue in the near future. See the Detailed Notes in the following chapters for more information and help with each of the Steps in the Fundamental Cycle.

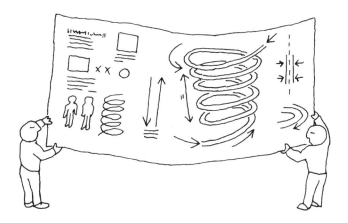

7 An Action Guide for Using the Fundamental Cycle

In the following chapters the Fundamental Cycle is laid out as a series of actions, Step by Step. The listing of actions shows clearly what should be done and when it should be done in each Step of the Cycle.

Following the actions for each Step are detailed notes for that Step. These notes provide a more thorough rationale and explanation for each action.

The Basic Steps of The Fundamental Cycle

1. Review your basic purpose.
Review your work unit's basic purpose. Why does the unit exist in your organization?

2. Set a direction.
Determine where your work unit as a whole and each of your immediate subordinates are going (targets, plans, budgets) during the next period.

3. Provide leadership.
Lead your work unit to make sure its targets are reached during the next period.

4. Learn from experience.
Make sure your direct subordinates review and learn from what was (or was not) accomplished by your work unit during the period.

Before proceeding with the action steps for the Cycle, you must decide how long your ''period'' will be—a month, two months, a quarter, six months, etc. Make that decision now.

8 Step 1: Review Your Basic Purpose

Purpose: To define what you and your work unit are responsible for and how your performance will be evaluated; also, to make sure your unit is organized appropriately for those responsibilities.

Actions

1. DEFINE what your unit is responsible for overall—in writing.

2. SPECIFY in writing how its performance will be evaluated.

3. DIVIDE your overall responsibility into its component parts. In general this division should follow the way you have assigned responsibility among your subordinates. (Unless you retain specific responsibilities yourself as an individual, the sum of your subordinate's responsibilities should equal your overall responsibilities as manager of the entire unit.)

4. SPECIFY how each subordinate's performance will be evaluated.

5. ASK YOURSELF: Is your work unit generally adequate to the work assigned to it? Does it have the necessary skills, people and other resources?

6. ASK YOURSELF: Is your work unit organized properly? (Drawing an organization chart can help here if more than a few people work for you.)

7. ASK YOURSELF: Does the match-up between people and jobs in your work unit make sense? Note any problems.

8. ASK YOURSELF: Does each direct subordinate understand his or her individual responsibilities? Note any problems.

9. GET AGREEMENT from your boss and subordinates about all of the above, if you have not already done so.

Detailed Notes For Step 1

The first step is to make an overall definition of your work unit's basic purpose. Why does it exist? The first part of that is to look at your own job. You must see it as a whole. Take special care, particularly if you are a new manager, to view your job as the sum total of all that you are responsible for (including the responsibilities of those reporting to you) and not simply what you do as an individual. Once you have defined your work as a whole, you need to break it down into its constituent major parts, which you probably delegate to those subordinates who report to you directly. Defining your responsibilities and getting everyone involved to agree on them, and how they are evaluated, is the basis for the rest of the Fundamental Cycle.

As a manager of people you cannot do all the work that is required of you; that is why you have people working for you. If you are a lower-level manager you will probably do some of the work yourself, but certainly not all. You will need to delegate responsibility. Delegation is a skill—in fact, one of the more difficult skills for a manager to learn. We sometimes feel guilty that we must ask someone else to do "our" work. We should not feel guilty. Delegation is at the heart of management; if we do not delegate, we are not managing. But be clear about this: we can delegate responsibility, but we cannot delegate accountability. Though we may tell a subordinate to do certain work, we are still responsible for seeing that the work is done and done properly. Our boss will hold us accountable, not the subordinate.

1. Define What Your Unit Is Responsible For.

Do not make more of this than it requires. What is needed here is about a 50-word or less statement of why your work unit exists in your organization. It should be as short and complete as possible.

2. Specify How Performance Will Be Evaluated.

Again, this relates only to your total responsibility, not its parts. How will the **overall** performance of your unit be evaluated—on what criteria? Sales, units produced, costs . . .? Be as concrete and specific as possible. There may be more than one criterion, or several criteria may be combined or related, so long as they all relate to the overall performance of your unit.

3. Define the Responsibilities of Each of Your Subordinates.

Do for each subordinate what you did for yourself. What is each subordinate accountable for? Be brief but complete. Your subordinates' responsibilities should add up to your overall responsibilities; that is, their responsibilities are the various components of your responsibility. If you were to start with your responsibilities and break them down into their various major sub-parts, those sub-parts should fall into position as the major responsibilities of your various direct subordinates. For example, the major areas of responsibility of a Marketing Director are usually advertising, sales, and product development; and the Marketing Director usually has subordinates who are responsible for each of those areas. (Sometimes a manager will retain personal responsibility for some parts of his or her overall responsibility. Our Marketing Director, for example, might delegate responsibility for advertising and sales but for some reason retain individual responsibility for product development. If that is the case with you, you will need to set targets and make plans and budgets for the areas you retain. You must plan as if you "report" to yourself, odd as that may sound.)

4. Specify How Each Subordinate's Performance Will Be Evaluated.

Do the same here for each subordinate that you did for yourself above. Answer the question: "What criteria will I use to evaluate the performance of each subordinate in each area of his/her responsibility?" Put your answers in writing. Be specific and concrete.

5. Ask Yourself: Does the Work Unit Possess/Have Available the Resources Necessary to Carry Out its Basic Purpose and Functions?

You must be satisfied that your unit has the necessary means for performing its basic job. Does it have the necessary number of people? The necessary equipment? The necessary space? The necessary overall time? The necessary funds in general? Be sure to include all tangible resources in your review. And, if appropriate, consider such intangible "resources" as visibility and status within the organization. The issue of resources, in my experience, is sometimes used as a crutch to explain lack of success, when resources are not the central problem. Yet it is true that a lack of resources can be fatal to any enterprise. Your purpose here is not to look at the adequacy of resources for any particular plan or project—simply at their overall sufficiency for your work unit's general purposes. A more specific look will come later.

6. Ask Yourself: Is the Unit Organized Properly?

All you need is common sense to answer this question—you do not need any special knowledge of organizations or organization theory. Does the organization make sense? (It may help to draw a simple organization chart here.) Are the responsibilities divided up in a logical way? It probably is not logical, for example, for one person to have two or more responsibilities which are totally unrelated to each other, unless that person is clearly designated as one who does two or more jobs.

7. Ask Yourself: Does the Matchup Between People and Jobs Make Sense?

This is a preliminary look at the relationship between jobs (and the skills and knowledge necessary to perform them) and people (with the skills and knowledge they have). At this point you need not be too detailed; just look in general at each position and at the person holding it. Look for obvious mismatches. If there are any, you will have to decide whether something needs to be done about it now. You can change the person or change the job. If you think there is a problem, talk to your boss and be prepared to make a recommendation. If there is a problem, or a potential problem, but nothing needs to be done about it immediately, simply make note of it; there will be opportunities later to deal with it.

8. Ask Yourself: Does Each Direct Subordinate Understand His/Her Responsibilities?

It is easy to assume that every employee understands what is expected of him or her. The easiest way to find out is to ask; show your subordinates the way you have broken down and assigned the responsibilities. That way, if there are any major disagreements, they can be settled now. Do not proceed beyond this point unless you are confident that your subordinates understand fully their responsibilities and what is expected of them.

9. Get Agreement from Your Boss and Subordinates about the Way Your Unit is Organized.

You may have chosen to talk to your boss at the beginning of this step; if so, that's fine. A discussion with him or her cannot be fully productive until you have something to discuss—which is the material you have been drafting up to this point. The discussion with your boss may produce revisions in what you have written until you have a statement which both of you can agree upon. It is critical that you reach agreement, and that both of you are satisfied.

It is equally important to get agreement from your subordinates at this point, though it may not seem so important now. If necessary, you can always "tell" subordinates what they are responsible for. But these are the people who must carry out the responsibilities and your job will be far, far easier if they and you agree from the beginning. But remember that you are ultimately accountable and therefore you must ultimately be satisfied.

Additional Notes

Get Help

Particularly if you are new to management, or to your current job, you should solicit help (opinions, advice, etc.) from several sources, including:
- your boss—he or she can be a major source of help, as well as the person who must finally approve what you write.
- people who use the results of your (your unit's) work.
- subordinates—talk out the overall responsibilities of your unit with them. Many or most of these responsibilities will eventually be delegated to them anyway.

Also, look at any written documents, such as job descriptions, policies, plans, etc.

Handling Pressure

Every job is the center of many pressures and demands. You will find a number of demands placed on you and your unit. All of them are not equally important but you may not be able to tell that from the pressure you feel. You will be able to deal with these pressures much more easily if you have defined, at the beginning, what you are responsible for, and how your performance will generally be evaluated.

After the First Time

After you have gone through the Fundamental Cycle at least once, this Step will be more a review than it is the first time. You certainly should review it with your boss, however briefly, each period. Every job is dynamic and if its basic responsibilities do not change from period to period, then the priorities probably will.

Don't Rush

You will be tempted to rush through this Step, especially after you have gone through it once. Do not belabor it, but do give it the necessary time and energy. If you have held your job for some time, but have never talked out your overall responsibilities with users or subordinates, or your boss, you should do that now.

Does It All Add Up?

Be sure that all the responsibilities you have defined and assigned in this Step cover all the work that needs to be done and for which your work unit is responsible. The Cycle will be perceived as useless if you leave anything important out.

Look At Your Own Responsibilities

If you "delegated" any of your responsibility to yourself as an individual, you must make sure that those responsibilities do not belong to someone else. For each one that you have assigned to yourself, make sure that it is logical and appropriate for you to do it. Are you taking it simply because you lack confidence in the subordinate who really should have it? If so, that is a separate problem you will have to face.

Matching People and Jobs

Most of us accept the idea of trying to match the abilities required by a job with the abilities possessed by the person chosen to do the job. There is a similar idea: that in selecting a subordinate you should also match the specific motivation pattern of the person selected with the ability of that job to satisfy specific motives. A motive is a need which a person wants to satisfy. By itself, a motive does not affect the way a person behaves. It is only when the need (motive) is combined with an opportunity for satisfaction that a person is motivated. Every job is different in the kinds of needs it can satisfy. Usually, a job can satisfy certain needs but not others. An obvious example: a person motivated by money will not find a public service job very interesting, because the job does not give him the opportunity of satisfying his need for money. Or, a job that offers little contact with people will hardly motivate someone who enjoys dealing with other people. So, when you look at a job and the person filling it, think not only of whether the person is able to do the job but also whether the person is willing to do the job—that is, whether the job is able to satisfy the person. Again, no great knowledge is required here. But it does require that you know the people who work for you and understand the nature of the work in each of the positions reporting to you.

The Importance of Clarity

For people to work their best and hardest, I believe they must feel personally responsible; that is, they must feel that if they do not concern themselves personally, the work will not be done properly. I believe this sense of responsibility is something that effective managers try to develop in subordinates. One of the key ingredients in a sense of responsibility is clarity—the perception of an employee that he knows what is expected of him. Clarity means that responsibilities are defined unambiguously. There seems to me a clear, logical relationship between clarity and the sense of personal responsibility. That sense cannot be high where the sense of clarity is not also high. When employees understand clearly what is expected of them, they are more likely to take personal responsibility for results. So, make sure that your subordinates know what is expected. Of course, expectations can and do change; situations change. That is why the definition of responsibilities is something that you need to look at and, if necessary, define anew frequently.

Try To Make Work Motivating

While you are looking at responsibilities and jobs overall, there is one other idea which needs to be raised. It is possible to motivate people through the work which they perform. If they find the work itself rewarding in some way, all the better. This kind of motivation is called "intrinsic" motivation—work is done because the worker likes to do it. The other kind of motivation is "extrinsic" motivation—where the reason for working is something apart from the work itself—pay or social status, for example. If motivation is extrinsic, then you as manager must continually find ways to motivate workers—more pay, more days off, and so on. Of course, motivation on the job is usually a combination of intrinsic and extrinsic; we like some parts of our jobs, but we work for the money, too. However, there are ways to structure work so that it is intrinsically more motivating. To the extent you can do that, you probably should. Look at the articles in Part III on making work motivating. Then, as you look at the way your work unit is organized, see if there are any ways the principles covered in those articles can be applied.

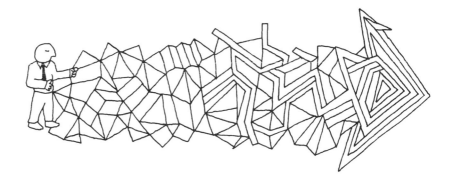

9 Step 2: Set a Direction

Purpose: To identify the specific accomplishments you and your work unit will achieve in the next period.

Actions

1. DEFINE a general direction and overall targets/standards for your work unit for the next period.

2. TRANSLATE these targets and direction into specific guidelines or expectations for each direct subordinate. Communicate these to each subordinate.

3. ASK your subordinates to set targets or standards for their areas of responsibility. REVIEW/CRITIQUE the targets or standards submitted and have them revised, if necessary.

4. SET developmental targets with each subordinate.

5. GET agreement from your boss on the targets or standards.

6. ASK subordinates to develop specific action plans for achieving targets or standards. (Decide which of these you need to review in detail.)

7. ASK subordinates to develop budget estimates for achieving each target or standard. Review these estimates and have them revised until they

are appropriate; then submit them in summary form to your boss. (See the Detailed Notes; a budget estimate may not be necessary for each period.)

8. COMMUNICATE the final targets and standards to others who need to know in your organization.

Detailed Notes for Step 2

It is not enough to define our responsibilities; we must also specify them in time. Thus your concern now should be, "What will my work unit accomplish in its responsibilities during the next period?"

Why set targets or standards? Because if we do not know where we are going, we are likely to end up anywhere, but probably not where we should be. And if we do not know where we are going, and what we specifically are trying to accomplish, we are not likely to convince anyone else, including our superiors, that what we are doing is worthwhile. Thus, setting targets serves several purposes: they make clear where we are going and why; they are a way to motivate ourselves and our work units; and they are a way to relate to our boss, for they tell him or her what we are up to and help make clear how he can help us. Having targets will help us determine for ourselves how well we are doing, and if the targets have been agreed upon by all concerned, they can serve as the basis for appraising our own performance.

But be clear about what targets are. Targets (or goals, or objectives) are a **statement of future position**. Setting a target says where we want to be at some specific time in the future. (That time, for our purposes, is either at or before the end of the next period.) The important point is, do not confuse targets with activities. Saying that we are going to do something is not the same as setting a target; a target says what we will accomplish—what will be done. This is a critical distinction because our responsibility as managers is the accomplishment of work, not the simple carrying out of some activity.

In some situations it may not be entirely appropriate to set targets, for what may be needed is the maintenance of a specified level of quality, rather than the achievement of a new level. In that case, we need to set standards of performance instead of targets. If you are responsible for the timely shipment of products, for example, and your unit has been shipping 75% of all orders within 48 hours, you might set a target of 90%. However, if 75% is sufficient and appropriate, you may simply set a standard that shipments will not drop below 75%. One might argue that targets and standards are essentially the same things. They are distinguished here only to emphasize that when we plan, we need to recognize the ongoing responsibilities of our work unit as well as the new or different responsibilities. The plans our units produce each period must encompass the full range of our responsibilities, not just a few of them. In the following pages, I often refer to both targets and standards. Keep in mind that any reference to one almost always could refer as easily to the other.

Because targets play such an important role in motivation, it is important that our subordinates, who will actually be working to achieve the targets, participate in setting the targets. A dictated target is better than no target at all, but a target which the person responsible has set or helped to set is even better. The person responsible must actually feel responsible. The Fundamental Cycle is built around targets and standards. Without them, it is useless. Yet the use of targets is laden with problems and potential problems. These are covered below. Be aware of the problems and work to avoid them.

1. Define an Overall Direction and Set Overall Targets and Standards for Your Unit for the Next Period.

This is where you act as a pathfinder and point to the proper direction for the next period. Choosing the right direction should be based on many things, including a strategic or other long-range plan (if you have one), and analysis of your performance in previous periods. You would be wise to enlist whatever help you can get in this activity from your boss, subordinates or any others. State your targets in the terms you used in Step 1 to define your unit's overall responsibility and the way performance would be evaluated. Also, the way a target is expressed is important. Make sure the way you have expressed each target satisfies the criteria below in the "Additional Notes."

Your work unit does not exist in a vacuum; it fits into a larger context. Thus, what you and your unit should accomplish will depend on what the rest of the organization is trying to accomplish. Understand the organizational context in which your targets will be set. Only your boss can give this to you. He/she may also refer you to other people or documents for further information. You may want to talk to your boss before you draft targets or a direction, but it is usually easier to talk about something definite, such as your written draft.

2. Translate the Direction and General Targets/Standards into Specific Expectations for Each Subordinate Reporting to You. Communicate These Expectations to Your Subordinates.

These expectations can be general, specific or both, depending on the level of experience and skill of each subordinate. For some you may only point a direction; you may tell others exactly what you want them to do. Again, base these expectations on long-term plans, an analysis of experience, input from subordinates, and guidance from your boss.

Your subordinates will soon be setting targets for their own work. They also need to know the context for their own targets. Let them know what you expect of them, individually, if you have not done so already. And let them know the general direction and overall targets you have set for the unit, if they do not know those already. Be sure your expectations cover all aspects of their work, including routine as well as special work.

3. Ask Your Subordinates to Set Targets or Standards. Review Them and Have Them Revised, if Necessary, until You Are Satisfied.

Be clear about what is needed from each subordinate. In some cases this may mean virtually telling subordinates what their target(s) ought to be; just be sure they are willing to accept such targets. Also, be clear about how you want the targets expressed; the way they are expressed can have an impact on whether they are achieved or not. The page later in this chapter entitled ''Questions To Ask Yourself To Make Sure Your Targets and Standards Will Be Effective'' can be photocopied for subordinates; it will help them judge their own targets before submitting them to you.

There should be at least one target or standard for each key responsibility held by a subordinate. In many cases it may be advisable to break these responsibilities down into their component parts and then to set targets for each.

Try to focus subordinates on what is really important. I am convinced it is better to have a few objectives which are pursued faithfully, rather than several which are pursued halfheartedly. It is your job to make sure this focusing occurs. However, if you do not include routine work in your expectations, you will have no idea of the overall workload you are placing on your subordinates. So include the whole job and focus on what is critical.

Review and critique the targets submitted. For each target or standard submitted you must ask five critical questions:

1. **Is this the right target?** Will it help the work unit achieve its overall target?

2. **Is it expressed properly,** judged by the criteria given below? In particular, does it say what should be accomplished (not simply an activity), and when it will be done (with interim checkpoints)?

3. **Does it fit properly** with other targets, both within the work unit and within the organization as a whole, so far as you know? Or, will it conflict with another target and so prevent either from being achieved?

4. **Is it the proper level of difficulty?** In order to be motivating, a target must be balanced between difficulty and ease. If too easy, it will provide no challenge and therefore no satisfaction if accomplished; if too difficult, the person responsible is likely to give up entirely, either immediately or at some later time. The phrase ''challenging but realistic'' sums up the level of difficulty needed.

5. **Does it use the strengths of the person responsible?** Or, does it assume that certain weaknesses will be overcome? As a general rule, I believe you should build on strength and avoid weakness. The best you should hope to

do with a weakness is to neutralize it. To assume it will be overcome is to plan to fail.

When you ask subordinates to revise targets, if that is necessary, be very clear and candid about what you want, and why. You should have high but reasonable expectations of what people can do. It may take more than one revision to obtain the targets that you want. If there is a target which you feel strongly is required, but a subordinate is hesitant to give, you may demand that target; but be aware of the potential problems in doing so and use the edict as a last resort.

4. Set Developmental Targets with Subordinates.

Make sure that in every case the person responsible for a target is in fact capable of achieving that target. Does he or she have the necessary skills, knowledge, and personality to succeed? If there is a serious problem, you should have caught it earlier, as part of your initial review of drafted targets. The point here is to identify any differences between the skills and knowledge required to achieve a target and those possessed by the person responsible. Where there is a difference, work with that subordinate to set an additional, developmental target which will close that difference. This developmental target should be added to the regular list of targets and treated as seriously as any other. If the difference is so large that you doubt it can be overcome, then you must ask whether that person should be in that job. The person or the job may have to be changed.

5. Get Agreement from Your Boss on the Targets and Standards.

Review the targets with your boss and get his/her agreement on them. The level of detail your boss wants to see will be up to him or her. At a minimum, get agreement on the targets for the overall performance of your unit.

6. Have Subordinates Develop Action Plans for Each Target or Standard.

For their own benefit subordinates should develop action plans for accomplishing their targets. You may or may not want to see these—again, it depends on the level of skill and experience of each subordinate. If there is much at stake, or the risk is high, or the subordinate is unable or inexperienced, you probably will want to review the action plan. It is the only way you can see if the subordinate has a reasonable chance of achieving the target.

7. Have Subordinates Develop Budgets for Each Target or Standard.

Every activity, personal and corporate, is constrained by limited resources. There is not enough money, time or people to do everything we would like to do. Thus every plan needs to have a budget—an estimate of the human, financial, and other resources required. You will not be able to have your targets and plans approved unless you have also estimated the overall cost.

Budgets serve not only to define the resources needed, but also to guide the revision of plans when all those resources cannot be obtained. It is an important part of your responsibility as a manager to ascertain that the resources available are sufficient to the objectives and functions at hand. This, unfortunately, can require at times that you have the wisdom of Solomon. When are resources truly "inadequate?" If certain work absolutely requires a specific piece of equipment, there is no question; without the equipment, the work cannot be done. But how do you know if a subordinate truly does not have the time to work on a project? There is usually no easy way to decide.

Whether budgeting is done in great detail each period will depend on how long your periods are and whether they match the budget cycle of your organization. At the very least each subordinate ought to look quickly at the resources needed for each target and verify that the resources (an already-existing budget, for example) are sufficient. If your unit does not already have a budget for the year, you and your subordinates should go through this step in some detail.

8. Communicate the Targets and Standards to Others

Let others in your organization (as identified or approved by your boss) know what your targets are. These are people who somehow depend on your unit or use its work in their work.

Additional Notes

Let Subordinates Participate

There are many ways for subordinates to participate in the setting of targets. The actions above call for the subordinates to draft their own targets, but that is not the only way. With some subordinates, you may want to work closely and even suggest targets. This is particularly true for new or inexperienced subordinates. In any case, it is important that subordinates come out of this process feeling a sense of "ownership" of their targets. Avoid the mere pretense of participation, which does not fool anyone (except perhaps you). True participation means that the subordinate will have had a genuine effect on what targets and standards were finally set.

Your Role

Besides setting the overall target(s) for the work unit and getting subordinates to agree to them, your key role in this step is to provide whatever help and guidance is needed. Work with subordinates to the extent necessary and to the degree desired by the subordinates. You are a resource, as well as the boss.

The Importance of Success

One of your goals here and throughout this Cycle is to make your subordinates successful. To the extent you can, you should keep those who work for you from failing. Making them avoid failure is not always possible or even advisable, but I believe that, as a general rule, failure breeds failure and success breeds success. The person who has succeeded will be more inclined to go on to more challenging things; the person who has failed will be inclined to try less and give up sooner. You want people to think of themselves as winners, not losers. Don't let people fail where you can avoid it. Of course, there are minimum standards, and what you must do is balance the need for success against those standards.

Problems with Targets and Standards

• The danger in setting clear, very explicit targets is that something will be missed in a job, particularly those parts of a job which are not easily reduced to clear, explicit targets. It is better to have some targets which are more vague than you might want, rather than have no targets at all. As you deal with higher and higher levels of management, goals tend to become more vague, or at least harder to quantify or make explicit. Setting effective goals is a difficult exercise. In setting goals, be sure that your have captured all of the job involved, and not just some parts.

• Setting targets is a skill which comes naturally to some people and not to others. As a skill it is something that can be learned and improved through practice. The point is, some people may need more help than others in setting targets.

• There is a negative side of setting targets. By defining success, targets also define failure. If someone does not achieve his targets, it will be clear to all involved that he has failed. That is not an argument for failing to set targets; it is an argument for setting them reasonably.

• It is too easy in setting targets to emphasize the short term. As the manager, you must make sure there is a balance in your own and your subordinates' targets between the short-term and the long-term. You should set targets or at least a general direction for at least a year into the future, and longer if possible. Obviously, you cannot see far into the future, but you must look hard enough to tell if there is something that must be done now to get ready.

• The ideal is to express targets as explicitly as possible, in measurable terms if possible. However, not all targets can be reduced to measurable terms. Try hard to quantify the results desired, but where it cannot be done, do not shrink from setting targets as best you can.

• It is easy and human to confuse targets with dreams, to mix what you would like to accomplish with what reasonably can be done. I think it is useful and appropriate to ask a great deal of yourself and those who work for you. But there is a limit. Consistently asking people to perform above the means available—time available, money available, or whatever—will simply burn them out.

Questions to Ask Yourself to Make Sure Your Targets and Standards Will Be Effective

1. Do the targets add up to your entire responsibilities for a given period of time? If not, targets must be added until, in total, they add up to cover the entire job. There should be at least one target (or standard of performance) for each major responsibility you have.

2. Are the targets the right ones, given the context of the work and the overall job that must be done?

3. Is each target as clear, concrete, and detailed as possible? If it can be expressed in numbers, use numbers. The point is to make performance against the goal as measurable as possible. Why? To avoid any future argument about whether the target was achieved or not. The less you must depend on anyone's judgment about whether the target was achieved, the better. However, do not avoid stating a legitimate target simply because it cannot be expressed in measurable terms. A nonmeasurable target is often better than no target at all.

4. Does each target have a deadline? If final accomplishment is some time away, it should also have some interim deadlines for measuring progress along the way.

5. Do all the targets fit with each other? Any conflict between targets will probably prevent you from reaching any of the targets involved. Resolve any conflicts.

6. Is each target reasonable? The ideal target is achievable, but challenging. Setting a target you clearly cannot achieve is worse than futile—it's demoralizing. Are there, or can you expect there will be, sufficient resources to reach the target?

7. Do you have the skills, knowledge, and inclination to achieve each of your targets? If not, you must either change the target or find some way to overcome your shortcoming.

8. Do not ignore long-term needs and opportunities in setting short-term targets. Get ready for the future.

Action Planning

What Is Action Planning?

Action planning is the determination of what must be done to accomplish the targets or maintain the standards that have been set. Action planning is the way you make the transition from defining where you want to be in the future (targets and standards) to deciding what you actually must **do** to get there.

As a means of shaping the future, the advantage of planning is obvious. But there are other advantages. Planning can increase the confidence and commitment of those doing the planning, for it makes clear exactly how a target will be reached. Planning is also an important tool for developing people. It can help develop two kinds of skills: the skill of planning itself, plus whatever skill is involved in the activity being planned. It is a particularly powerful method of development because it provides an opportunity for a subordinate to work through a future activity without risk. There is no risk because the activity is entirely mental. A mistake in planning is harmless, assuming it is corrected before the plan is implemented.

Planning is not a natural activity for most people. My experience says it is one of those activities that nearly everyone says is important, but few people actually take the time to do. I understand some interesting experiments have shown that even in situations where planning is obviously advantageous, it is usually not done because current tasks and problems take all available time. That probably applies to this Cycle as a whole. None of it will happen by itself; you must make it happen.

Later in this chapter there is a section entitled ''Questions to Ask Yourself to Make Sure Your Action Plans Will Be Effective.'' If you wish, make copies of this section and give them to your subordinates as they prepare their plans; it will help them review their own plans before submitting them to you.

Your Role

Be clear about your role here. It is not to make the plans yourself (except those, if any, for yourself as an individual). Your primary role is to make sure there are adequate plans in place to insure the successful accomplishment of your unit's targets. Thus your primary role as your subordinates develop action plans is to act as a resource, a guide, one who makes sure the plans are prepared in such a way that they have the greatest chance of success. As a practical matter, you will not, and should not, see an action plan for every target a subordinate sets—only those of special interest, where the subordinate is inexperienced or untested, or where much is at risk.

Critiquing Plans

How you critique a subordinate's plans, particularly those of a relatively inexperienced subordinate, is important. The key is usually not to "tell" the subordinate anything but to ask the right questions. Planning involves judgment and judgment is not something that can be told. The kind of questions that are often most effective are the "what if?" questions—what if this happens? What if that happens? What if that person does not agree? What if the response is less than you expect? Plans necessarily are based on assumptions, which may or may not be reasonable. The "what if?" questions are a way of testing those assumptions and the subordinate's ability to be flexible. In the end, if you feel strongly enough that a certain assumption is wrong, and the subordinate simply does not agree, you may have to exercise your authority to change it. Do not be afraid to change it—indeed, you must. But there is always the risk that you will be wrong.

Look for the Strategy

The greatest danger in reviewing a plan is that you will become lost in the details; in a typical plan you may see dozens of different activities prescribed. Where should you start your review? The first thing you should always look for is the strategy or rationale behind the plan. Consider an obvious example: if your goal is to sell 55 cars in the next three months, and your plan only talks about such things as hiring more salesmen, and putting more models in the showroom, something is missing. What is missing is some statement, explicit or clearly implied, about what it takes to get 55 people to buy cars. Will you do it with price? If so, then certain kinds of actions fall out of that approach. Or will you do it by stressing dependability and service? If so, certain other actions fall out of that approach. In short, you usually cannot do everything and must make choices. While the action plan must say what you are going to do, it must also say somehow why you (the person preparing the plan) think those actions will achieve the target. That statement is the strategy. And that is what you as the manager must look for in a subordinate's plan. Once you have found it, and determined that it is reasonable, you can review the planned activities themselves and decide whether they will adequately carry out the strategy. Thus, an action plan should contain two elements: a strategy which is a general statement of how (by what kinds of activities) the target will be reached, and a list of timed and coordinated activities which will implement the strategy.

Build in Controls

Every complete plan must specify how it will be controlled; that is, how will the person in charge be able to tell if the plan is being implemented as you wish? Of course, the key thing is to be able to tell if the target is being accomplished; you must be able to measure progress toward the target. But you will also want to tell if the plan is being followed. Those two pieces of information will then tell you if the plan is working, i.e., taking you toward the target. So, be sure that each plan includes some statement of how it will be controlled. This may consist entirely of a list of checkpoints, by which time certain actions will be done. Or, it might be more elaborate. In any case, be sure the method of control is one that allows the person carrying out the plan to control himself. (See the Detailed Notes on control systems in Chapter 10.)

Is Change Involved?

If the action plan is one that calls for changes in the way things are normally done, then be aware that the plan may encounter resistance from those who want to continue the old ways. For some ideas about how to handle this resistance, see the article in Part III on change.

Level of Detail Needed

The level of detail required in a plan will depend on several things, primarily the experience and skill of the person who will implement the plan. A skilled and experienced person may be so familiar with the actions involved that he need do little besides identify some checkpoints. On the other hand, an unskilled or inexperienced person will need to lay out a strategy and proposed actions in great detail. When you instruct your subordinates to make action plans, tell each one the level of detail you expect. Other factors determining the level of detail include: the risk involved and the cost of failure, and the newness of the activity or target, regardless of the skill and experience of the person involved. When the risk is high, you will want to see a detailed plan, even if it involves activities done many times before. If the work involved is new, though the person is very experienced, you may still want to see a detailed plan. In the end, the level of detail required will depend on your judgment of what is needed to make sure the targets are reached.

Use for Development

This point is worth repeating: Use these action plans for development. Planning will give the inexperienced subordinate a chance to make mental dry runs at no risk. So, make development a part of the action plan.

Questions To Ask Yourself To Make Sure Your Action Plans Will Be Effective

1. An effective plan contains two key elements: a strategy and a set of coordinated actions. The strategy is a statement, implicit or explicit, of how the target will be reached—of what general kinds of activities will lead to success. It is the business equivalent of the ''game plan'' in sports. The activities are thus a consequence of the strategy. So: Is your strategy a reasonable one? Does it have a good chance of accomplishing the goal? Are the activities noted the right ones for carrying out your strategy?

2. Is the action plan built on your strengths? Or, does it assume that weaknesses will be overcome? Always build on strength and plan, at best, to neutralize or circumvent weaknesses.

3. Is the action plan reasonable? Can it be done within the limit of the resources available?

4. Does your action plan specify who will do what, when? It should not be vague about the people involved, or about what they will be doing, or when they will be doing it.

5. Are there clear, definite checkpoints for making sure your plan is being implemented, and determining whether the plan is actually accomplishing the target?

6. Does your plan fit with other plans? Or do different plans, for example, require the use of the same resource at the same time? Make sure that the planned activities do not conflict.

7. Is the plan in writing, even if it is brief?

8. Does your plan identify any obstacles or risks involved and specify how they will be dealt with?

9. Does your plan list the major assumptions on which it is based? These may be important for deciding later whether or not to change the plan.

Detailed Notes on Budgeting

Budget = Set of Spending Targets

The budget is nothing more nor less than a set of targets expressed in dollars or some other resource. The budget is a statement that you or your subordinates must accomplish something at a specified cost. It is not simply an accountant's tool; it is an important manager's tool, too. Even if you do not do a detailed budget every period, you still should satisfy yourself that adequate resources of all kinds are available.

Be Clear about the Budget Rules

The rules vary in every organization. Find out what they are in yours. They cover not only what specific accounts you should use, and the format for presentation, but also what freedom is given to those who have budget responsibility. Once money is approved for a given line item (e.g., travel), is the person in charge of that budget free to use that money for some other purpose (e.g., supplies) in his budget, so long as the total budget is not exceeded? Some organizations say yes, and others say no. Are you accountable for monthly budgets, or primarily for quarterly or even yearly budgets? When is a variance from a budget serious? 5%, 10%, 15%? What is your spending authority and the authority of your subordinates? As you learn these rules, communicate them to your subordinates. Remember that in many cases you may have freedom to vary them within your unit, so long as your unit as a whole conforms. Talk to your boss about that.

Fitting This Cycle to Your Organization

You may be starting on this Cycle for your unit at a time when your organization is not actively preparing a budget. For example, your organization may be on an October-to-September fiscal year, which means it will be preparing an annual budget in July, August, and September. What if you want to start this Cycle in December? You can do that (and should, if you want to), but realize that you will already have a budget that you must live with for the rest of the current fiscal year. At the end of next summer you will be able to integrate this Cycle and your organization's budget process. Until then, do your best. Your boss can help here.

Planning Is an Iterative Process

Don't be discouraged if you prepare a budget and discover that your plans simply cost too much and you must cut them back. That is the reason for budgeting—better to find out now than to start implementing a plan and have to cut it back in the middle. With experience, as you develop targets and action plans, you will be able to tell whether they will be too expensive. Usually all that will be required is to modify the plans slightly. Just be aware that it is normal to work through a plan several times before it is satisfactory.

Pay Attention to Format

By format, I mean the way budget information is laid out on the page. The format will imply the level of detail needed. Be very clear about the format you want your subordinates to follow in submitting their budget requests. If they all follow the same format, the requests will be easy to read and compare. If your organization does not already require a certain format, you will have to designate one. Your boss can help here.

Find Out How Budget Reports Will Be Made

Most organizations issue monthly reports that show how much has actually been spent versus the amount budgeted, by month, by quarter, and year-to-date. Find out about these reports in your organization. Also, find out how the reports are organized. Will there be one report for your entire work unit, or will there be several? If several, how will they be organized? Most accounting systems are flexible enough that the reports can be changed, if you let the accounting department know what you want (and why) before the start of the new fiscal year. Again, you will need your boss's support.

Budget All Resources

Budget not only dollars but also other resources needed: people (by position and type of position); capital expenditures, space, and so on. You need to develop a list of all the important resources needed to carry out a plan.

10 Step 3: Provide Leadership

Purpose: To lead your work unit so it can successfully implement the plans, and achieve the targets, set in Step 2.

Actions

1. ENTER on a calendar all the checkpoints from your subordinates' targets/standards and plans.

2. IDENTIFY the information/analysis needed to keep track of targets and plans, then make sure it is developed.

3. SCHEDULE regular meetings with subordinates to review progress.

4. KEEP TRACK of progress as subordinates implement their plans during the period, by means of the checkpoints, information/analysis, and meetings noted above.

5. REVISE targets and plans, or reallocate resources, when absolutely necessary.

6. PREPARE periodic written reports on the progress of your unit as a whole.

7. BEGIN planning for the next period. Prepare Steps 1 and 2 of the Cycle, so they will be completed by the beginning of the next period.

Detailed Notes for Step 3

This Step is the reason the whole Cycle exists, for it is here that the work gets done. Since we managers are not the ones doing the actual work, we must be careful to follow the action steps below. What we need first is to define how we will keep track of our unit's plans and our progress in carrying the steps out. We want to make sure that our work units are doing what we said we were going to do, that our actions are having the results we wanted. "Making sure" is another name for control, and what we need now is some way of maintaining control—making sure that what is supposed to happen does, in fact, happen.

Well, you say, things do change. The future may not turn out to be exactly as we assumed. That's true. It is also the most powerful argument possible for making plans and having a control system. The only way to know what you need to do is to know where you want to go and where you are now. You cannot know those things unless you set targets or standards and measure performance against them, even though you may change them several times.

1. Enter on a Calendar All the Checkpoints from Your Subordinates' Targets and Plans.

It may be a special calendar you use only for this purpose, or it can be your regular calendar. (Put any checkpoints from your own targets and plans on it, too.) These notations will make it easy to see when things are supposed to happen, and to find out if they do happen.

2. Identify the Information/Analysis Needed to Keep Track of Targets and Plans—Make Sure It Will Be Provided.

Do this for every target/plan you and your subordinates developed. For some it will only be a single piece of information (e.g., sales); for others it may be several pieces. For each piece, you must also identify:

- Where it will come from
- How it will be calculated
- How it will be presented
- Who will be responsible for it, and
- How often it will be developed.

Keep a written record of all those decisions. Enter any dates on your calendar. Add the responsibility for the information to the plans of the persons designated as responsible.

3. Schedule Regular Meetings with Subordinates To Review Progress.

You cannot keep track of everything with checkpoints and information on paper. You will still need to depend on the judgment and interpretations of those who work for you. Thus, you will need to meet with them face-to-face. You may want to meet regularly with individuals, or with groups, or both. Schedule these meetings and enter them on your calendar; treat them as seriously as you would any other commitment.

There should be nothing secret about the way you keep control. A subordinate should know that she will be meeting with you every Friday at 3:00, for example, to review her four targets. Try to coordinate such meetings with the availability of information (from Detailed Note 2 above). Be clear about your control system; that will enable your subordinates to develop their own control systems which will fit with yours. It will give the subordinates a chance to control themselves.

4. Keep Track of Progress as Subordinates Implement Their Plans During the Period.

Do all those things here that you decided to do in the previous Step to keep track of how well the plans were being implemented and whether the targets were being reached. This includes keeping track of checkpoints, receiving and reviewing information and analysis, and meeting with subordinates. Keep track in writing of how well you follow this schedule, so at the end of the period you can review how well the control schedule worked and revise it for the next period. If you plan to meet frequently enough with individual subordinates, you can build most of these control steps around those meetings.

Help your subordinates. Never forget that once the planning is done and the implementing has started, one of your key tasks as manager is to help make sure your subordinates succeed. In any rational organization you will rise on their shoulders, and they will rise on their subordinates' shoulders. As your subordinates succeed, so will you; and as they fail, so will you.

5. Revise Targets and Plans as Necessary.

As you and your subordinates gain experience during the period with the targets and plans, the question will certainly arise: Should you revise targets and plans? The answer is, Yes, under certain circumstances. The guiding principle here is this: Keep the targets and plans challenging, but realistic. If it becomes clear that a target, for example, is impossible, it should be changed because it will have lost its ability to challenge and motivate. But if you are too willing to revise a target, simply when the going gets tough, no one will take targets seriously in the future. Thus, you should be willing to change targets, but only when the evidence is clear that the current target is not realistic at all. The rule I use is this: Be willing but slow to change targets, but be much more willing to change action plans. The purpose of an action plan is to achieve a target; if experience tells you there is a better way than the one you first planned, then change to the better way. Just be sure that the "better" way is really better. Test it if you can before committing yourself to it. And change your plans based on good sense and solid evidence, not fear or panic because initial results are not as positive as you had hoped. In the same way, be willing to move resources around as you gain experience.

6. Prepare Periodic Written Reports.

At reasonable intervals (e.g., monthly) prepare brief reports on the progress your work unit is making as a whole, working toward the overall targets and standards you set. The purpose of this report is to say in one place how everything is going. It will force you to take a broad look at how your unit is doing; it will keep you from spending all your time focusing on one or two troublesome areas.

Give the report to your boss and go over it in person with him/her. This will give you a chance to talk about any problems or changes all at once. Your boss will probably like the bird's-eye view. There are good reasons your direct subordinates should probably see the report, too. It will tell them how the unit, of which they are a part, is doing. It will give them the broader context of their work. You should also give copies of the report to any other people in the organization who need to know (as suggested or approved by your boss).

7. Begin Planning for the Next Period.

Prepare a time schedule for completing the first two Steps of the Cycle and then prepare them for the next period, so that they are at least drafted by the start of the next period. This means you will have to do the planning for the next period before this period ends. It cannot be helped. Once the period ends and you have reviewed results for the period, you and your subordinates can make final adjustments in the plans for the next period (which will have already started). If you wait until the period ends and you have reviewed results before starting work on plans for the new period, you will be far into that period before the planning steps for it are done. Better to overlap periods so that when each new period starts, you will be ready for it.

Additional Notes

Self-Control

None of us really likes to be controlled by someone else. I think that, as a general rule, people prefer to keep track of themselves and their own progress, so that they can make any necessary adjustments without being told. This presents a problem for you: How can you maintain the kind of control you want without making subordinates feel you are watching them too closely? First, as noted above, be clear about what kind of control you want (what do you want to know, and when, for example). This will give the subordinate a chance to negotiate with you, or suggest alternatives that may satisfy both of you. Second, in every way possible, let the subordinate control himself or herself. This does not mean you give the subordinate complete freedom. The subordinate is still accountable. It does mean that the subordinate will have the information and ability to track his or her own progress and initiate, within limits, any adjustments needed. Self-control is thus control in two stages. The first stage is the one where the subordinate can monitor himself and make changes. If you have set it up properly, you will have much of the same information the subordinate has, so you can see what he is doing (but without telling him anything directly). The second stage occurs if the subordinate has failed to make his own changes, even though he has had the opportunity. Then you must step in and make whatever changes you think are necessary. At least the subordinate will have had the chance to control himself.

Keep Written Records

I have found it useful to keep some kind of written log of progress—of checkpoints made or missed, of changes made, of discussions and decisions made at meetings. At some point you may want to go back and reconstruct the sequence of events—for the performance appraisal, for example. In some cases you might ask for brief written reports from your subordinates—a couple of lines each week on each target/plan, for example. Try to set up such measures so subordinates can use them to keep track of themselves, and let you know the results.

Follow the Plans

Let me say it again: Follow the targets and plans you have made. If you must change them, as we discussed above, then change them. But make the changes in relation to what was planned before. If you simply forget the plans, you will find that planning is difficult in the future, because no one will take it seriously. If circumstances occasionally require a change in plans, then be candid with your people about why the change is necessary. As long as it does not happen frequently, changing plans is not a problem. This may seem like an obvious point, but you will be surprised how easy it is to simply forget the plans.

Use Flexible Delegation

I believe that one of the key management skills needed to rise in management is the skill of delegation—the ability to pass responsibility to subordinates and still get results. Be aware that there are degrees of delegation, ranging from full and complete delegation to very limited delegation (delegation on a short rein). It may help you to think of four different kinds of delegation:

Do it yourself: This method of delegation is not really delegation at all, though you do assign a task to a subordinate. In this case you will do the task yourself, while the subordinate watches or assists but takes no major role himself. In this type of delegation, you are setting an example, showing how, and you make all the decisions and handle all the problems.

Be the director: In this type of delegation the subordinate plays a more important role, but you (the manager) remain the more critical participant. Here, you decide what should be done (you dictate the planning) and you direct the subordinate in detail. The subordinate does the actual work, but under your close supervision.

Be the catalyst: In this type of delegation you lay out the task and the objectives involved, then, through questioning and discussion, make certain the subordinate is considering all the major issues and problems involved. Beyond that, you allow the subordinate to make decisions and handle problems, and to carry out the delegated task himself. You are a catalyst in this situation because you make things happen, but do not participate directly in them yourself.

Be the overseer: Here, you hardly become involved in the delegated task at all, once you have assigned it and made sure the subordinate understands what is required. The subordinate will make all the decisions and handle all the problems himself. You will become involved only if there is a problem that requires your help, and to review progress periodically.

These degrees of delegation can be used for specific, limited delegated tasks, or as a general approach to the Fundamental Cycle. The level of delegation you use with a subordinate will depend on the skill, knowledge, experience, and dependability of that subordinate. It can also depend on the specific task or tasks involved, for the skill or knowledge level of the subordinate can vary with the type of task involved. It is part of the judgment you must develop as a manager to know which kind of delegation is appropriate with a given subordinate at a given time.

Signs of Overcontrol

There are certain indications which appear when subordinates perceive management control to be too extensive or heavyhanded. They include:

Bureaucratic behavior: Here people work exactly "according to the book." They do exactly what they are told and nothing more nor less. Obviously, every contingency cannot be anticipated and you must depend on people's judgment and discretion. If subordinates feel that you are overcontrolling them, they will say, in effect, "OK. We'll play your little game. We'll do exactly what you say, exactly how you say to do it, but nothing more. See how you like that." You probably will not like it, and there will be little you can do about it because people will only be doing what you said to do. As a general rule, use the minimum control necessary, but no less. And make sure the subordinates involved understand the controls and can use them on themselves, rather than waiting for you to tell them what is right or wrong.

Useless information: Under extreme conditions, where control is rigid and the stakes are very high, there may be a tendency for subordinates to produce useless information when reporting on their work. By "useless" I mean information which is, at worst, false, or more likely, wishful rather than realistic. The best example of this is that people will often tell you, with good intentions, merely what you want to hear. This kind of situation is likely to occur when a) the determination of work quality is defined by you alone (or someone else other than those actually doing the work), b) there are no clear objectives, c) the data for evaluating results is all subjective and judgmental, and d) rewards are entirely tied to the control system and there is no latitude for adjusting rewards.

Outright resistance: Subordinates may complain that the controls are too tight or rigid, or the resistance may take the form of quietly grudging acceptance. Usually people need a period of time to become accustomed to the controls; that is why a new control system should be introduced gradually. You are also likely to have better luck with overcoming resistance if subordinates are approached from this point of view—let subordinates control themselves, with you watching and intervening only if there is a problem that is not being handled adequately. You should control the controls.

This Cycle has been set up to avoid as much as possible these problems, but they cannot be avoided entirely. Be aware of them.

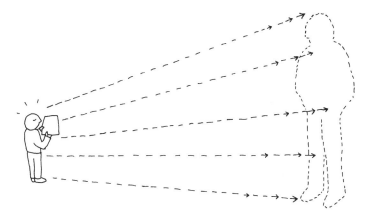

11 Step 4: Learn from Experience

Purpose: To learn and improve by reviewing what was and was not accomplished during the last period, and why.

Actions

1. REVIEW your unit's overall performance (and your own as a manager)—write a final report for the period.

2. ASK each subordinate to appraise his/her own performance for the period in writing.

3. MEET with each subordinate and discuss his/her performance. Before each meeting, decide upon your own appraisal of the subordinate's performance. Reach agreement on ways the subordinate can improve.

4. REVIEW your overall report and the individual appraisals with your boss.

5. MAKE any final adjustments in the plans for the new period just beginning.

Detailed Notes for Step 4

The final Step in the Cycle is an obvious one; it is to look back at the period you and your work unit just finished and try to learn from it. I believe the only reason for ever looking back is to improve performance in the future. It is an obvious point, but I find that I must remind myself of it constantly. If you observe it faithfully you will find, for example, that it makes a dramatic difference in the way you conduct performance appraisals.

1. Review Your Unit's Performance and Write a Final Report.

As soon as possible after the end of the period, review the work that was done during the period against the targets (or standards and plans) that were set at the beginning of the period. The key question is: were the targets achieved? If the targets were not accomplished, what was the problem and how can it be avoided in the future? This final report is not basically different from the periodic reports you wrote during the period, except that it covers the whole period and should contain a summary of what was learned for future reference.

2. Ask Subordinates To Appraise Their Own Performance.

Ask those who report to you to evaluate their own performance during the last period. Ask them to concentrate on what they actually accomplished versus their targets or standards. Ask for these evaluations in writing. The evaluations should include an analysis of the reasons for not reaching any targets.

3. Meet With Each Subordinate and Review His or Her Performance.

Your organization may only require a formal appraisal of performance once a year. However, a study done at General Electric found that an annual appraisal is not frequent enough; it has little effect on performance. Thus, the Fundamental Cycle calls for one at the end of each period. What should happen in this appraisal is that you sit one-on-one with each subordinate and review the subordinate's performance during the period against the targets and plans that had been set at the beginning. Be sure to discuss any development targets and plans that had been made and whether or not they were achieved. The gist of this appraisal should be: What was learned about the subordinate's skills and knowledge, strengths and weaknesses, that can improve performance in the future? Where there are weaknesses, discuss how they can be neutralized or overcome in the future. Note any that need to be added to the targets and plans for the next period. Be sure to discuss strengths. How can they be made even stronger? How can they be used more advantageously? In short, what was learned about the subordinate in the period that can help the subordinate do better in the future? (See Additional Notes below and the related articles on appraisals in Part III.)

This meeting can be even more useful if it includes some discussion of your performance as the subordinate's manager—that is, did you help the subordinate or did you in some ways (probably without intending to) hinder his performance? You might want to ask simply, ''Are there any additional ways I can help you?'' or, ''Have you ever felt that the way I managed you was not as helpful as it could have been?''

You or the subordinate should write a summary of each appraisal. Note what was discussed—where you agreed and disagreed. Note anything that was decided; any plans made or development targets set. Note the subordinate's strengths and weaknesses. If you have set any conditions on future employment, you should probably write the summary yourself and be sure to note those conditions. You, your subordinate, and the subordinate's personnel file should receive copies. If the subordinate writes the summary, be sure it includes everything pertinent.

4. Review Your Report and Appraisals with Your Boss.

This is the final action to close the period. Discuss the period with your boss. He or she may or may not be interested in the details of your appraisals with subordinates. Give as much detail as desired. In effect, this meeting should be your own quarterly appraisal. Talk about where you succeeded and failed during the period, and about where you need to improve. If anything worth noting comes out of this meeting, make a written summary afterwards for yourself and your boss. Finally, distribute copies of the report to your subordinates and others in the organization suggested or approved by your boss; this, of course, does not include the appraisals (each subordinate should receive a copy of his/her own appraisal).

5. Make Any Adjustments in Plans for the Current Period.

You and your subordinates developed your basic plans for the current period during the latter part of the last period. If your appraisals of unit and individual performance after the end of that period indicate the need for any changes in plans for the new period, you should make those changes as soon as possible.

Additional Notes

Conducting an Appraisal

Detailed notes for conducting an appraisal are contained in Chapter 24 (''Appraising Employees''). Be sure to read that chapter, as well as the one on leveling (Chapter 23). Some highlights are worth repeating here:

• Again, the purpose of an appraisal is to improve future performance. If a problem has nothing to do with future performance, forget it.

• The purpose of an appraisal is not for you to get something off your chest that might be bothering you about the subordinate. It is not to make you feel better. Improving future performance—that is the only purpose of a performance appraisal.

• The appraisal interview is not an adversary proceeding, with each person trying to win the upper hand and put the other on the defensive. It is an investigation of ways that the subordinate can improve his or her performance. You should both be seeking the same goal.

• That does not mean you and the subordinate will always agree. You will not. Just be sure that the subordinate knows and understands your point of view; be sure you understand his or hers.

• As much as possible, judge performance against the targets or standards that were set. The clearer, more objective, more comprehensive those goals were, the easier the appraisal will be. In the ideal appraisal, the targets will have been so clear, and performance so obvious, that the subordinate can obviously appraise himself. Things are never that neat, but do your best to work toward it.

• Always keep the appraisal discussion on a professional level. You are appraising the work of the person, not the person himself. You are not qualified to pass personal judgment; it's not part of your job anyway. Discuss personality traits (intelligence, initiative, aggressiveness, charm and so on) only as they relate directly to the current or future work. Otherwise, stay away from them.

• Always support the integrity and self-worth of the person being appraised. You may criticize what someone has done, but you should not criticize the person himself. Try to maintain that distinction between the person and his or her behavior; talk about behavior, not the person.

Marginal or Inadequate Performance

People need to know where they stand. If their performance has been barely adequate or inadequate, you must tell them so, in enough detail that they can improve, if possible. Be clear about how long they have to improve. Do all you can to help them improve. Then, if improvement is not forthcoming, you must remove them from the work they are doing. The extreme alternative is to fire them. It may come to that. But also consider transferring them to a job which might use their strengths better, if such a job exists. Also consider changing the job. Jobs and organizations should not be built entirely around the particular individuals involved, but there is always some flexibility in defining a job. See the relevant articles in Part III on working with a marginal performer and on firing an employee.

PART III
SOLVING PROBLEMS

12 The Manager as Leader

In nearly all cases, a collection of people needs leadership, I believe, to be completely effective as a group. A leader in this case is one who sets or clarifies direction and maintains the group on its course. Such leadership may be formal or informal. Where a formal leader has not been designated, one probably will emerge from the interaction of the group members. Formal or informal, leadership is crucial.

Is the manager a leader? Yes, he (or she) is, or, at least should be, if he is to be effective. What is the difference between a manager and a leader? A manager is the one formally designated to set direction. A true leader is one to whom people look for direction. Thus, the leader and manager may be the same person, or they may not be. Ideally, the one formally designated to set direction is also the one to whom people look for direction. But this ideal is not always the reality.

One of our functions as managers is to set direction for the groups we lead. Can we perform this function of pathfinding without truly acting as leaders? Only partially, I think. To find the right course does not necessarily require leadership, but to lead others on that course obviously does. Thus, if we wish to manage effectively, we must be able to lead, and to that end it will help us to know something about leadership.

Consider an example: An acquaintance of mine entered an organization to take a new management position several years ago. His department included 23 people, divided into three sections, with each section headed by a manager reporting to him directly. He had never before seen any of these people. The three managers under him had each wanted the position he held. (This was similar to the problem Martin faced in the case in Part I.) No one knew of this person's coming until the day of his arrival. They were all surprised and angry because each of them had felt himself best qualified. The immediate problem this acquaintance faced, besides all the problems of the job itself, was to find some basis for managing these three key subordinates. "Well, he was the boss," you might say; he was the boss because the organization said he was. True enough, but was that really a sufficient basis for leadership? In fact, it was not though, at first, he adopted that approach. The response of the three managers was to accept him, but only formally. He obtained grudging obedience with the letter of his directives, but not the spirit. That may have sufficed with hourly workers; it was obviously inadequate with higher-level subordinates upon whose judgment he had to depend.

The real question for this fellow (and for every manager) is this: On what basis does an effective manager/leader build his relationship with those who are supposed to follow?

Why Do People Follow?

Important as it is, leadership is not a one-way relationship. Those who follow are seldom a group of sheep willing to be led anywhere. A leader by definition influences the followers, but followers also influence leaders. The leader who ignores this influence for too long will find himself no longer accepted as leader; while he might remain leader in title for a long time, his ability to lead effectively will be severely diminished.

People follow because the leader possesses authority which they are personally willing to accept as legitimate. Where does the manager/leader get that authority? The obvious answer is, from the organization. But the answer is not really as simple as that, for there are different kinds of authority. They include:

Formal authority: This is the authority that someone possesses by virtue of his or her formal position in an organization. A follower accepts this authority because it has been granted by the organization that both the manager/leader and the subordinate/follower work for. If the follower wishes to remain in the organization, he must accept the official leader.

Authority of being an expert: Here, someone is leader because he or she possesses knowledge and skills beyond those possessed by the followers. The followers accept leadership in this case because the leader knows more than they do and they recognize the importance of that knowledge. Followers may believe a leader possesses expert authority because of the leader's training, experience, reputation, or demonstrated ability.

Charismatic authority: Here, followers accept a leader because they identify personally with him or her. The leader represents values, standards or characteristics that are important to them. They accept this kind of leader as their spokesman and representative. They accept the leader's authority because they believe that by accepting it they will support and strengthen further their own values and beliefs. This kind of leader is able to lead because those who follow want him to lead and have designated him leader in some formal or informal way.

Sources of Authority

The different types of authority come from different sources. The power to hand out rewards and punishments, which is the essence of formal authority, usually comes from the organization that the leader and follower belong to.

However, expert and charismatic power do not (in fact, cannot) come from the organization. They spring from the leader himself: his or her mind and personality. In these cases, the leader must earn the authority to lead by means of what he is or does.

Researchers have found that if they set up a group of people, all of whom are basically peers, and give them a task, a leader will usually emerge spontaneously. And, in most cases, this leadership will be based on either charismatic authority or expert authority, or both. In such groups, the group members may themselves grant formal authority to the expert or charismatic leader in order to reinforce his position.

Using Different Sources

Think about someone you know who is a leader, including yourself or your boss. Many leaders in fact possess more than one source of power. Most managers have authority to reward and punish, at least within certain limits. Managers, by definition, are given formal power by the organization. Many managers possess the authority of knowledge or expertise for at least a portion of their work. And many managers develop and use charismatic authority in their relationships with subordinates.

You might find it useful to consider which sources you actually possess in your current position and which you tend to use most. (Of course, you can possess more than one type of authority.)

Think of the sources of authority as tools. Most of us tend to follow a pattern or style in the way we use the different kinds of authority we have. We may demand obedience because we are the formal leader; we will not tolerate any disagreement or insubordination. We may tend to use rewards or punishments as a means of getting what we want ... the carrot and stick approach. Or, we may demand obedience because we are the expert and, in a given situation, we know best.

In fact, the skillful manager uses his or her different sources of authority creatively, depending on the followers involved and the situation itself. Followers, as individuals, have different affinities or aversions to the various kinds of authority. One person may dislike the formal authority figure, but would be willing to accept the authority of an expert. A manager might persuade this individual to do something by appealing to superior experience or knowledge, without using the authority inherent in his formal position. Another individual may doubt his manager's superior knowledge, but may be willing to accept his manager as the one possessing formal authority.

The most difficult type of authority to use explicitly is charismatic authority. Here the follower follows, but for less tangible reasons. The other forms of authority can be used explicitly. As manager, you can actually lay them out for a subordinate by explaining, in effect, that you are the boss or that you are the expert. But you cannot really say, ''Follow me because I am charismatic, because I represent this group and I stand for all the things it believes in, because you identify with me.'' These things can all be implied, but probably not stated explicitly.

Leadership based on charismatic authority is the most difficult type of leadership to understand, but it is real. Every effective political and religious leader has had it. And most really effective managers have it. Some have it more than others. It has much to do with respect, but almost nothing to do with being nice or likable. Nor does it have anything to do with being socially outgoing or personally showy.

I believe the wise manager possesses as many different types of authority as possible, and knows when and with whom to use each one.

Leadership and Performance

There has been some research into the relationship between the performance of subordinates and the type of leadership used. The different types of authority seem to have different effects on performance. The results are not conclusive by any means, but are offered here because they seem to make sense. The use of formal authority will get the minimum job done. By using the authority given by the organization, the manager can motivate people to do a job to the minimum standard. However, formal authority seems not to be sufficient in most cases to get people to work at higher-than-average levels of effectiveness.

The use of leadership authority based on expert knowledge or charisma seems to be best at getting high performance from subordinates. Subordinates are apparently more willing to work at a maximum level when they are urged on by a leader who knows more than they do, or whom they have personally adopted as their leader.

That, in fact, was what my acquaintance finally did. He did not know as much technically as the three key subordinates (one, for example, was an accountant), but he discovered that all were frustrated that they had no influence in the organization. The acquaintance knew how to develop a base of influence in the organization and so was able to make the subordinates more effective; eventually they accepted him as leader based on this kind of expert knowledge. It took time, but it worked.

13 Helping Subordinates Learn

As managers, we must possess a variety of skills. I am convinced that one of them is the skill to help people learn. We are not teachers—not in the sense of a classroom teacher conducting a formal learning session. But on the job there are everyday situations in which subordinates need to learn something—new knowledge, such as a new billing procedure, or a new skill, such as how to upgrade a sale. We often find ourselves teaching the employee, if only in an informal way.

For one of our subordinates to increase his skills usually requires him to learn something. If we are managing that subordinate's overall development, we must supervise the subordinate's learning, for development and learning cannot be separated.

To be effective managers, I believe we must see ourselves as teachers—informal teachers, even teachers by accident or necessity, but teachers nonetheless. So the question of how people learn and how a manager can facilitate learning is of critical importance to effective management.

How Do People Learn?

What is learning? Without becoming entirely tangled in that question, let's simply take a practical definition: learning is new behavior, the ability to do something new. This definition may not cover all possible learning situations, but in the typical job, it will probably cover 99% of all the cases you will find.

How does learning occur? What is the process of learning?

There is a simple model of how learning occurs. It is useful because it can be applied to a wide variety of situations you are likely to encounter as a manager. According to this model, learning is goal-oriented and proceeds by trial-and-error. It can be illustrated this way:

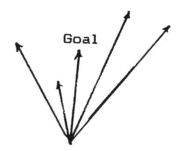

Learning does not occur, or does not occur as well, unless there is a goal expressed that the learner is trying to achieve. The way the learner learns—that is, accomplishes the goal by doing something new–is by repeated efforts, initially unsuccessful, but gradually more successful, closer and closer to the goal. Eventually, through this trial-and-error method, the learner reaches the goal and is able to do something that he was unable to do before.

What the Model Means

When you reflect on the model it becomes clear that learning will usually occur more quickly and more effectively when it is managed. In some cases, the learner is his own best manager, but typically, management best comes from someone else—such as you, the manager.

The manager's task is first to establish a clear learning goal, and then to supervise the trial-and-error efforts of the subordinate.

Setting the Goal

What do you want the subordinate/learner to be able to do? What is the new behavior? A key part of setting the learning goal is to define how you and the subordinate will know when he or she has reached that goal. What are the criteria for success? How many times must he do the new behavior? How quickly? How accurately? Under what conditions? These criteria should be as objective as possible to avoid misunderstandings later.

As manager, it is your task to set the goal. However, it is clear that allowing the subordinate/learner to participate in setting the goal is desirable. It will increase the learner's motivation, and in many cases can speed up the learning process. Obviously, the learning goal must be something the subordinate wants to learn.

Managing the Trial-and-Error Efforts

Learning occurs better under some conditions than others. So, to help you manage the process of trial-and-error, I have summarized a number of these conditions from the research about how people learn:

• Learning requires the freedom to fail. If the subordinate is not able to make repeated attempts (failures), the goal may never be reached. You must recognize that failure will occur and you must create a situation where failure is acceptable, at least temporarily.

• It is also important that you create a situation in which the subordinate/learner is ultimately successful. This does not conflict with the first point. The subordinate must be able to fail, in order to succeed eventually. Set realistic goals. If necessary, set a number of successive goals, instead of one goal that is too challenging. Learning should be a process of proceeding from success to success, with intermediate trial-and-error stages. Otherwise, the subordinate will soon become dissatisfied and demotivated.

• The learner must be motivated to learn. This may involve explaining why the new behavior is important; it may mean involving the learner in defining precisely what the new behavior will be.

• Work-related learning is most successful when it comes directly out of the work to be done. **You should organize work so that it requires learning.** One way is to make developmental assignments—assignments which require the subordinate to learn something new in order to carry out the assignment successfully. Learning should be part of the work to be done.

• Learning should start from the subordinate's current position of skill and knowledge. It is easier to go from the known to the unknown, than from the unknown or unfamiliar to the unknown.

• Learning something entirely new can be easier than learning to do something familiar in a new way. Learning can be more difficult when an established pattern of behavior must be changed.

• Encourage the subordinate/learner to use other, related knowledge he or she may already possess. The subordinate may know other things which can be translated to the field you are dealing with.

• People learn at different rates and learning progress is seldom steady. It often moves in great leaps, and then comes to a temporary halt or plateau.

• People also learn in different ways. Some prefer to read; some prefer to listen. Some prefer to try something very quickly; others prefer to understand thoroughly before they try it at all. In any case, it is clear that adults learn more effectively when they can learn at their own pace and in the way they prefer.

• Different kinds of learning require different times and methods. Simple subjects, such as motor skills and memorizing, can be learned most quickly. It takes a bit longer to learn to adapt, or to gain and apply new knowledge. Next in difficulty is learning new ways of dealing with other people. And hardest of all is to learn new values—that is, to overcome prejudices. The simplest kinds of learning can often be handled by simple reading or explaining. But the more difficult kinds require much trial and error.

• A critical element in the learning process is that the subordinate/learner must receive constant feedback. Remember the model. As one attempt fails, the learner will not be able to make a closer attempt the next time unless he or she is given information about how successful the previous attempt was. Ideally, the learning situation is set up so that the learner can obtain this information for himself.

A Checklist

Here is a simple checklist you may want to use each time you determine that a subordinate needs to learn something:

1. Is there a clear goal expressed in concrete, behavioral terms? That is, does the goal state what the subordinate will be able to do after learning?

2. Is it clearly stated how the subordinate will demonstrate that he or she has accomplished the learning goal? What are the conditions under which the newly-learned behavior must be demonstrated?

3. Are the amount of time and effort you expect to devote really sufficient, given the type and difficulty of learning involved?

4. Have you defined how the learner's behavior will be evaluated? Who will evaluate it? Can they evaluate it themselves?

5. Have you created a situation where there is freedom to fail in order to learn? How long does the learner have to make repeated but unsuccessful attempts? What is the deadline for learning? The learner should be aware of the deadline.

14 Making an Assignment

One of the more disconcerting experiences we can have as managers is to ask a subordinate for a particular piece of work and then get something which is not quite what we asked for. I suspect this occurs at every level of management, from the lowest to the highest. We make an assignment which to us is perfectly clear. The subordinate gives every indication it is also clear to him or her. Yet when the work is done, it is clear that either he did not understand what we had in mind, or he was not able to produce what we wanted.

Sadly, our occasional failure to get what we want from subordinates is probably our own fault. We simply fail to make assignments properly. There are no secrets to making assignments effectively. It is one of those activities where we need to remember the basics now and then, and make sure we are doing the simple things that help insure success.

Effective Assignment Making

I define effective assignment making as the assignment of a task in a way that helps insure the successful completion of the task. In asking yourself whether you are making a particular assignment effectively, there are only four basic questions:

1. Is the assignment clear?
2. Is the subordinate able to carry it out?
3. Is the subordinate motivated to carry it out?
4. Can you manage the assignment properly?

Is It Clear?

Common sense tells us people are unlikely to take responsibility unless it is clear what they are responsible for. If, in the mind of the subordinate, you have not clearly conveyed what you want, he will probably take the assignment lightly, or will attempt to fill in the gaps himself and thus misinterpret what you want.

Specifically, what does it mean to say an assignment was clear? Ask these key questions:

Is the goal of the assignment clear? What specific results do you expect?

Is it clear how the results will be evaluated? What would be good results? Adequate results? Inadequate results?

Does the subordinate have the necessary background information to carry out the assignment? Is there a context or perspective in which the assignment fits, and without which the assignment does not make sense? There are times when we would like people simply to do what we say and not worry about why. But, by and large, people do want to know the larger context in which they work, and seem to work better when they understand it.

Is the subordinate aware of any necessary guidelines or restraints which apply to this assignment? There may be limits, such as a budget or company policy. Is the subordinate aware of these?

Is the priority of the assignment clear in relation to other work? Perhaps you will get what you want, but will you get it when you want it? If there is a deadline, does the subordinate know it? If there is, is it realistic and believable? Is the subordinate aware of any drop-dead date—the absolute deadline?

Is the Subordinate Able?

Does the subordinate know enough? Does he or she have enough knowledge, training or experience to do what you want?

Does the subordinate possess the necessary skills or experience?

Will the subordinate have the necessary help, if help is required? If it is, will it be up to the subordinate to identify the need for help and actually get the help himself? Or will you, or someone else, help him identify the need and make clear it is acceptable to ask for assistance? Will you help identify places where help might be obtained?

Is the Subordinate Motivated?

Does the subordinate think the assignment is important?

Is the assignment a complete task? Does it have a beginning, middle, and end? Is there an end-product which the subordinate will be able to point to and say, "That is something I accomplished?" In short, is it something from which he or she can obtain satisfaction?

Most assignments have an end-product of some sort, and somebody is going to use that end-product. (If not, you might well ask what the point of the assignment is.) The recipient of the end-product might be you and/or someone else. Does the subordinate understand how important that end-product is to the end-user? Does he or she have any contact with the user? Or, will he simply complete the assignment in a vacuum, unaware of who will use it or how it will be used?

Will you communicate your high hopes and expectations for this assignment to the subordinate? You cannot assume because you are making the assignment that the subordinate will automatically understand what is on your mind.

Are you making the assignment in writing? Or, for example, will you make it when you run into the subordinate in the hallway, as an afterthought? The setting for making an assignment can convey a clear message about the assignment's importance.

What is the probability of success for the assignment? If too high or too low, that will tend to demotivate many people. There usually needs to be some difficulty involved, but only a moderate amount. A probability of success somewhere around 50/50 seems to be the most motivating level of risk, at least for those who take pleasure in accomplishment.

Can You Manage the Assignment?

In most cases you simply cannot assign the task and then forget it—much as you might like to. Usually you must follow up in some way, which includes the following:

Will you monitor the status of the assignment? Are there checkpoints, formal or informal, at which you could determine whether the employee is making progress or not? Even if the assignment is a trivial one that does not merit a formal or written plan, you nonetheless should have in mind a rough timetable and convey that to the subordinate.

Will you doublecheck to make sure that the subordinate seeks and obtains help if he needs it? Some people accept a difficult assignment as a challenge and, to them, the need for any help indicates a weakness, even though they may fail without help.

Do you plan to manage the assignment in a way that is appropriate to the skill or knowledge level of the subordinate? If the assignment involves something new and strange to the subordinate, will you maintain frequent contact and provide sufficient help? Conversely, if the assignment is something that the subordinate should be able to do with a minimum of direction, will you constantly look over his or her shoulder? That can demotivate, and irritate too.

A Common Cause of Error

In my experience, the problem is often that an assignment simply evolves into being. At first, the need for it is small and ill-defined. Then, as the situation develops, the need for it grows. As a result, the assignment is never explicitly and fully stated to the subordinate. To avoid this, you must identify the situation as one definitely requiring an assignment, and then make the assignment formally and explicitly.

The Importance of Assignments for Development

If you use the required daily work to develop people, you will find that one of the key methods for doing this is through the daily work assignments you make. Listed above are all those elements which need to be present if an assignment is to be completed successfully. But, in many cases, you do not need to make all of them explicit, because they may be clear from the situation itself or from the subordinate's experience. However, if you often make assignments for the purpose of developing someone, you are more likely to make assignments to people who are less familiar with the work to be done. (If you always assign work to someone who is very experienced, you need not explain a great deal, but the assignment will not help that person grow in the job.) Thus you cannot assume as much knowledge and experience on their part. Someone for whom an assignment is a developmental experience will have a strong need for the assignments to be especially clear and explicit.

15 Managing Change Effectively

All of us know managers who believe that if only they knew the right tricks they could make subordinates do anything. Unfortunately (for them), effective management is **not** a bag of tricks. I believe the manager who manipulates may succeed for a time, but generally not a long time.

The failure of management by manipulation becomes most apparent in trying to institute change in an organization. There are no tricks with which we may entice or fool subordinates into genuinely accepting change.

However, because organizations often change and managers must constantly face the problem of resistance to change, it is legitimate to ask: How can we as managers introduce change in a way that is most likely to gain genuine acceptance?

It is not a matter of fooling or manipulating anyone, but of instituting the change in a way that encourages subordinates to accept it, live with it, and make it work.

Resistance to Change

Conventional widsom says people always resist change. The implication is that there is nothing you can do about this resistance, so why bother worrying about it? As with most generalities, there is some truth in this, but clearly it is not true for everyone in all situations. Do you know any adults who want to eat hamburger for every meal? Or even steak? Do you know anyone who wants to work every day, with never a weekend or vacation off?

Probably not. And if you do, you probably consider them oddballs. So, it is not that people resist change, but that they resist certain kinds of change.

What seems clear to me from my own reading and experience is this: **When people do not control the change or its consequences, or do not participate in the making of the change, they are likely to resist.**

I suspect the reason for the resistance is usually a basic one—fear. Fear of how the change may affect them and their jobs and their friends and their status and their income. Recognize that this is a gut-level issue with many people, and that their resistance may far outweigh in intensity the scope of the change itself.

The fear can take many forms, ranging from outright hostile resistance, through quiet resistance and sabotage in subtle ways, to silent, sullen acceptance. The resistance may be entirely unspoken—to you, anyway. Remember that even when you change someone's behavior, you are not automatically changing what is in his or her mind. The result is that you may get the change you want, but the old behavior will return at the first opportunity.

Steps for Successful Change

Making a successful change is really a process, I've found, not a single event. It is a series of interrelated steps. All the key people involved in the change must pass through these steps if the change is to be effective. If you are spearheading the change, you must make sure all the steps are taken and all the key people are involved. This is true even for small, less important changes, as well as major organizational changes.

The steps in the process of change are identifiable:

1. **Recognize the need for change.** Pressure must build based on the difference between the actual situation and what people think it should be. Change is more likely to occur when this pressure develops both from outside the organization (from customers, for example) and from inside (from other people or units within the organization). At the same time, those who need to change must not be able to blame their problems on someone or something else.

2. **Define the need.** This involves gathering information and defining the problem in detail. At this stage, as many people who will be involved in the change should be consulted as possible. If you alone define the need, and do not involve those who will be affected by the change, you are not likely to find strong support for the actual change when it is implemented. On the other hand, if you delegate the change to subordinates in a completely non-directive way, the subordinates are likely to question your real interest in having the change occur.

3. **Find a solution.** Continue the process of definition by finding alternative solutions to the problems and needs defined in the previous step.

The difficulty here is to resist the natural temptation to use the same old solution for a new problem. If a problem is new, it may need a new solution. On the other hand, "back to basics" is sometimes the right answer, too. The simple point is to be aware of the need to define whether the problem is old or new.

No one can plan a change and then figure out how to make the change appealing. It is far simpler to take into consideration the appeal when planning the change itself. The appeal should be built in, not added on.

Make sure the people undergoing the change have the ability and skills necessary to carry out the change. Training, or retraining, may be necessary.

4. Try out the solution. No one knows whether a recommended solution will work until it has been tried. Test the solution. Instead of making a big change all at once, make a series of small changes in gradual steps. These are trial runs which let you adjust as you go along. There are obvious exceptions where rapid change is necessary, but in general there are real advantages in starting slowly.

It may be possible to simulate the change, even before trying to implement it. Try it out as a game or in some way that does not involve any risk. If you are changing the way orders are processed, for example, introduce dummy orders and have them processed in the new way to see if there are any problems.

5. Put the change in place. Positive results from trying out the solutions can produce a strong reinforcing effect. As the solution begins to work, people will see its advantages. At that point you can put it into final place. The key here is to have a plan for implementation, with goals and deadlines.

Research has been done into self-directed change, in which an individual or group decides for itself that it should change. The research centered on what makes this kind of change successful. Two elements were critical: **goal-setting**—the definition of what specific change should occur and the setting of goals for attaining that change; and **feedback**—as the effort to change is underway, those changing must receive concrete information about their progress in achieving the goals. Where there are goals and feedback, both the commitment to change and the likelihood that change will in fact occur are much higher.

Change should be undertaken in a timely way. It should not be forced quickly. On the other hand, once you have determined the specific change to make and have tested it, you should move expeditiously. There should not be a time when everyone waits and wonders what will happen next. This is one of the reasons for setting deadlines and developing a plan for implementation.

Change often produces conflict. To prevent this conflict from sabotaging the change, it must be confronted and settled quickly and directly by you, the manager.

I believe it is implicit in all these steps that successful change must be actively managed, not simply dictated or allowed to run its course.

Sudden Change

In spite of the best intentions, there will always be situations where change must be implemented which cannot be discussed beforehand and must be "sold" to those involved afterwards. Here are some pointers on how to make the best of such a not-very-good situation:

• The highest managers involved in making and implementing the change should be personally involved in explaining the change to those affected through face-to-face communications. This personal contact cannot be delegated, nor can it be done well by memo or videotape. The personal touch all the way down the line is important.

• Those explaining the change should not overestimate the appeal of logic in making their explanations. Again, resistance to change is not always a logical matter.

• Appeal to the values and legitimate self-interest of the people affected. Try to see it through their eyes and seek out those aspects which to them are most important and appealing.

• Above all, be clear and complete as possible in talking about the change. And be honest. If some aspect is not yet settled, say so if you can. Lying never helps and destroys whatever credibility you might have had.

• Where distasteful change is necessary, go through the above steps, then make the change as quickly, cleanly, and fairly as possible.

• If it is appropriate in your organization, appoint someone to be the lightning rod for complaints and problems. Announce that person as the one employees should see with questions and gripes. This will help you fully gauge resistance and plan any further steps.

16 Communicating as a Manager

Communication refers to the sharing of information, feelings, and opinions between two or more persons. When done successfully it leads to shared understanding. Two people have truly communicated if they both understand what the other knows or feels. It does not mean that they necessarily agree; they simply understand one another.

Obviously, effective communication is critically important to successful management. The problem is that in an organization (with its many levels of authority), the organization itself has a profound impact on communication. We need to be aware of this impact, as well as some other fundamental concepts of communications, in order to manage effectively.

Communicating in Organizations

In general, as messages pass through different communicators, they are inadvertantly altered by the omission, addition or distortion of information. Communication in an organization is not quite the same as communication in other settings. Messages in an organization can move up and down, as well as sideways.

Of particular interest to you as a manager is the phenomenon of distortion—that, as messages move up or down the organization, they tend to be distorted because they are moving from one status level to a different status level. People at the higher level generally have control over those at lower levels—they evaluate their performance and determine whether they will retain their jobs or receive various rewards. Those at the lower level consequently tend to seek the approval of those at the higher level. The result is that, as messages move up the organization, any bad news is either removed or downplayed. That is why those at higher levels tend only to hear good news and not bad; if they want the bad, they literally must seek it out. On the other hand, good news tends to move up the organization much more quickly and to receive inordinate attention.

This problem is aggravated by the tendency for those at different status levels to interact with each other less than those at the same level. (Bad news travels sideways quickly in an organization.) Interaction between levels not only tends to be less, but also more formal. The result is that, to the extent interaction is necessary for good communication, communication will be worse between levels than it is within levels. In concrete terms, this means that there are fewer questions asked between levels, and less informal discussion. Many times these questions are critically important if a message is to be conveyed accurately; the person receiving the message may need to ask several questions to clarify what he or she is hearing; indeed, the questions may be necessary for the message-sender to clarify in his own mind what message he is trying to send.

In addition to the relative lack of free and informal interaction between levels, there is an additional problem with messages moving **down** an organization. Those at lower levels are likely to attach too much significance to what they hear from higher levels. Thus a manager may discover that some innocent remark he made to a subordinate as part of small talk in the hall has suddenly flown around the department as official news. This of course aggravates the problem of low interaction between levels. The manager burned by his small talk is thereafter guarded about what he says to those below him.

Nonetheless, I would argue that the relationship between manager and subordinate should be as open as possible. There should be a great deal of informal, two-way interaction—questions, answers, and open discussion. If communication is not open, there is less opportunity to work out in detail the meanings that each level is trying to convey to the other. Both manager and subordinate need to be able to convey more information than the absolute minimum and each side needs to feel able to ask questions when necessary.

There seems to be some evidence that where manager and subordinate are open with each other, the subordinate is more likely to feel satisfied with his work and organization. An interesting result of this study is that the amount of mutual openness seems to depend more on the manager than the subordinate; that is, the manager determines the nature of the relationship.

The point is that if you wish to use openness to prevent the problems of communications between levels in the organization, it will be up to you as manager to establish that policy and set the example.

A Philosophy of Open Communication

Complete openness is obviously not the answer. You cannot tell everyone everything. Some information is personal, some information is so uncertain it would only cause confusion if spread around, and some information is confidential for competitive reasons. Because it is so difficult in many cases to determine which information to share, and which not, many managers adopt the philosophy that subordinates should only be told what is necessary for them to perform their jobs. This is the "need to know" approach.

The "need to know" approach is at the opposite end of the communication spectrum from the open approach. You may favor one approach over the other in general, but deciding whether to pass on a particular message is always a matter of judgment, to be decided case by case. There is no easy way to make this decision. Those who favor "need to know" can always point to problems caused by handing out too much information. Those who support openness can point to problems caused by too little communication. So, consider two guidelines for deciding what information to communicate:

First, when deciding whether or not to communicate, you should ask yourself "Why not?" If there is no good reason not to communicate, then you probably should communicate. Those who favor the "need to know" approach generally ask themselves "Why?" and refuse to communicate unless there is a compelling reason to do so. That approach can reduce communication almost to nothing. So, ask yourself "Why not?" instead of "Why?" whenever the question of communicating a specific message arises.

Second, the important question is not—What does someone need to know just to carry out the activities of his job? Instead, it is—What does someone need to know to be motivated to do his job well?

To think through this distinction and answer the real question requires some of the concepts that have emerged from research on job enrichment. An employee tends to be more motivated when his or her job is whole: that is, when it has a beginning, middle, and an end; and, above all, when it produces a clearly defined end-product of value. For example, someone performing one small activity in the assembly of a product is less likely to be motivated than someone assembling the whole product, or a whole sub-assembly. An essential part of being able to see one's job as a whole activity with value is to understand the context in which it is performed, and to understand the needs and reactions of those who use the end-product. (Do they like it or not?) For an employee to have this kind of perspective requires more information than is allowed under a simple "need to know" approach. Thus, you should ask yourself, whenever a question of communication comes up—Will this information help my subordinate understand his or her whole job better; why it is done the way it is; why it is important; and what the reactions of the "customer" for his end-product are? If the answer is "yes" to any of these, then you probably should communicate the message in question—again, unless there is a compelling reason not to. The application of this guideline will not always be simple, but it should be worth trying nonetheless.

Nonverbal Communication

Nonverbal communication refers to messages conveyed in some way other than the spoken or written word—by facial expression, tone of voice, body posture, gesture, clothing, and so on. There are some points concerning nonverbal communication that you need to know because they affect the way you manage and communicate.

• You can choose not to speak or write, but you cannot avoid nonverbal expression. Silence itself may convey a message. So what you are "saying" nonverbally is not something you can ignore. You are always communicating, one way or another, and you ought to be conscious of the messages you send.

• Nonverbal messages tend to convey feelings, attitudes, and reactions, as opposed to facts and concrete information.

• Nonverbal messages are more believable than the written or spoken word. For example, if someone asks if you like something, and you say, "I like it," but your facial expression and tone of voice say, "I can't stand it," the listener will probably believe your expression and tone, not your words. At the very least, he will be confused about what you really mean. It is relatively easy to tell a lie with your mouth or pen, but unless you are an accomplished actor, it is almost impossible to lie with nonverbal expressions. Perhaps that is why people tend to believe them.

You must take great care that the messages you convey verbally and nonverbally are the same. If you say you want bright, innovative ideas, but day-to-day the only thing you ever pay attention to are expenses, you will get people who spend most of their time on meeting the budget and not developing new ideas. Someone has referred to this phenomenon as the "words and music" of an organization. People dance to the music, not the words.

I believe that open, two-way communication is the best remedy for this problem. If there is open communication between two persons, and one of them receives a mixed message, he (or she) will feel free to ask why there is a difference between the verbal and nonverbal elements. The open discussion should clear up any problems or misunderstandings.

17 People and Decision-Making

Making decisions is clearly a fundamental task of managers. Indeed, some writers have called decision-making the activity which distinguishes management from other functions in an organization.

Decision-making is simply the choice of one alternative from among several choices—one of which is always to do nothing. That sounds deceptively simple, but we all know that it can be terrifyingly difficult.

The purpose here is not to talk now about how to make decisions, but to discuss our role as managers in making decisions. As managers we neither work alone nor make decisions alone, though we do have to assume sole responsibility. So it makes sense to think about decision-making in the context of managing.

The Decision-Making Process

The actual making of a decision is really the final step in a series of steps. Those steps include:

- Defining the problem
- Defining the criteria for making a decision
- Defining the various alternatives available
- Forecasting the outcomes under each alternative
- Making the actual decision.

You surely have seen those steps enumerated one place or another. Aristotle probably had something to say about them. They are listed here only to make the point that it is indeed a process, and not a single activity.

You may not go through that process formally every time you make a decision; some situations are so familiar that the process is almost unconscious.

It is easy to forget that decision-making is a series of steps and to think of it in total as the manager's sole prerogative—something you must do alone. Surely the final step is indeed your responsibility, as it is your responsibility to manage the process and take responsibility for the outcome. But there is nothing that says you must undertake all the steps in the process alone. In fact, I suspect the manager who consistently does them all by himself is probably a fool who makes poor decisions.

I believe the key point is this: You can improve the quality of your decisions by improving any one of the steps in the decision-making process.

Problems in Decision-Making

Consider all the problems that can arise in the decision-making process. Usually a poor decision is not something that simply happens mysteriously; it is the result of something that went wrong with one of the steps prior to the decision itself.

First, there is a human tendency to define a problem too quickly. We may assume that we know what it is, that it is like some other problem we already understand. In fact, we usually want to define a problem this way because that makes the problem familiar. In addition, we often define something as the problem which is actually a symptom of another, more fundamental problem. The danger here is that treating the symptom will not ultimately solve the problem.

The converse can also occur in defining a problem: the defining can go on forever, so that a decision is never made. Where the problem is unusually difficult, the temptation is to keep on looking for more and more information, for that one clue which will make the proper decision obvious. Except in rare cases, such a clue does not exist—at least you will probably never find it. Gathering information, especially the right information, is critical to good decision-making; but after a certain point, the gathering of more and more information does not help. It only delays getting to the actual decision.

Defining the decision criteria and all the real alternatives, as well as forecasting the possible outcomes, are all difficult activities. What makes decisions particularly susceptible to error is bias, the individual point of view, that all of us bring to decision-making (and everything else in life). Bias not only affects what information we gather, it also affects the way we interpret that information—the criteria, alternatives, and outcomes we define as part of decision-making.

I suspect that we tend more naturally to make a ''no-go'' decision, rather than a ''go'' decision—perhaps because a ''no-go'' decision is safer. If it is wrong, it will seldom be obvious.

In addition, research indicates that decisions made under stress tend to be poorer that those made in less tense circumstances.

And, finally, an obvious problem, but one worth noting: it is easy to overlook conflict and other problems which can result from a decision. Where the consequences on people are concerned, it is too easy to review possible consequences from the point of view of how people "should" react, rather than how they will actually react. Better to deal with reality, unpleasant as it might be sometimes, than to fool ourselves.

Implications for Decision-Making

I think the primary implication of what has been said so far is that **you are probably better off involving those who work for you in the process of making decisions that affect them.**

There are obvious disadvantages of such participation—it may generate conflict, cause people to put pressure on you, the decision-maker, and it will certainly take more time than if you shut your office door and do it all yourself.

In most cases, however, I believe the positive effects of involving people will ultimately outweigh the bad. If the decision must be implemented by those people, involving them is more likely to insure their willing help. But most important of all, involving people in the steps prior to the actual decision will usually lead to better decisions.

Why is that so?

Gathering enough of the right information concerning a problem, and being able to view it as clearly as possible, are necessary preliminaries to making effective decisions. By involving others (assuming they have something relevant to say about the topic) you can increase the chances that the right information will be gathered, and you will insure enough different points of view that individual biases—including your own—will be cancelled out. This approach to decision-making has been called the "problem-solving" approach.

The Problem-Solving Approach

Think about the way you usually make a decision (or solve a problem) and then about the way you implement what you have decided. If you are like most other managers, as revealed by research, you probably decide what you want to do, then call all those involved together and "sell" your decision. That is, you try to persuade the people, by reviewing whatever data seems relevant to you, that your decision was the right one. If the decision was a controversial one, you probably will get some argument and, finally, grudging acceptance.

With this selling approach, you may have problems getting people to implement your solution with any enthusiasm. Do not underestimate the importance of that enthusiasm; in many cases, the decision finally made is almost irrelevant, in that many different decisions could work, so long as they are implemented with energy, enthusiasm, and intelligence.

In fact, the "sales" approach to decision-making is bound to aggravate all the problems enumerated a moment ago that can occur in making decisions. The manager who undertakes the decision process alone, and then tries to persuade others that he (or she) has made the right decision faces two problems: he is limited only to the information he possesses or can find himself, and he has no way of countering whatever biases he holds.

In my experience, where there is conflict over the proper decision, the best decision is often an integration, a creative combining of different points of view. This is not the same as a simple compromise where all sides win a little and lose a little. An integrated solution is one which combines the best elements of the conflicting sides, but in a new, innovative way that none of the sides would have found by themselves.

The way to improve your chances of finding such a solution is through the problem-solving approach, as opposed to the sales approach.

The way to use this approach is: instead of gathering the people involved and explaining why your solution is best, gather them, present the problem (not your solution) and share any (and all) data you have; then discuss alternatives. What you will often get from the resulting discussion are alternatives which you had never thought of and which will, in fact, work better than what you, or any of the other people involved, might have produced alone.

None of this reduces your ultimate accountability for the quality of the decision; but that is precisely the reason you should consider the problem-solving approach. Not only does this approach often produce better alternatives and therefore better decisions, but it also tends to lead to decisions which are better accepted and more willingly implemented by the people involved.

18 Brief Notes on Promoting People

Not everyone is promotable (by definition, most people cannot be), nor is there opportunity to promote everyone. But for those who are promotable, you may want to work with them on development plans that will prepare them for advancement. Such plans should contain these specific steps:

1. Identify the position or positions for which the employee might be considered; the employee's own goals and inclinations are obviously of great importance here. Identifying such positions does not imply a guarantee of promotion—only the possibility.

2. Do an analysis of what specific skills, knowledge, and experience the employee must develop to be promotable to the positions identified. This analysis is done by comparing what skills, knowledge, and experience the promotion-position requires versus what the employee already possesses.

3. Based on that analysis, identify the gaps between what that position requires and what the employee already possesses. Those gaps will probably need to be filled before the employee is fully promotable.

4. Plan ways the employee can close the gaps. This development plan can easily be integrated (and should be) into the Fundamental Cycle. Through all of this process be candid with every employee: no promotion is guaranteed. Going through these steps does not constitute a promise of promotion.

Going through these simple steps for more than one employee may help you decide which one should be promoted. The key point to consider in promotions is this: a promotion should go to the person best able to perform the new job, and not necessarily to the one who has performed best in the prior job. In most organizations there is not necessarily a natural progression from job to job. The skills required in one job may not be the skills required in the job immediately above it. For example, the best engineer does not necessarily make the best manager of engineers because the skills of managing and those of engineering are very different. A promotion is a reward for good performance in a previous job **only if the new and old jobs are similar**. The promotion should not be used as a reward if the jobs are different.

Take care that an employee does not assume that good performance in a job will automatically lead to a promotion. It may or may not, depending on the specific jobs involved. Be clear about what is required for promotion.

19 Managing to Develop People

The development of employees is one of the themes I have consciously woven through this book. Developing people—increasing their ability to work well—is one of the more important tasks we must perform as managers.

Unfortunately, development of people is one of those activities which we frequently put off, no matter how important we say it is. I have found it useful to ask myself periodically whether I am doing everything I can to develop those who work for me.

Asking that question really involves asking three questions:

1. Am I encouraging people to develop themselves?
2. Is the development of my subordinates being consciously pursued so that it occurs in consciously chosen directions?
3. Am I actually taking steps to help subordinates develop themselves?

Are You Encouraging Subordinates to Develop Themselves?

It is almost a cliché, but it is nonetheless profoundly true: No one can develop anyone except himself. All development is self-development. Your purpose as manager is to foster the employee's own desire to develop and grow. You must be the catalyst—the agent that causes something to happen.

You can encourage people to develop themselves in many ways, but all those ways have one common characteristic: they create a gap in the mind of the subordinate between what he (or she) is and what he should or could be.

In short, all those ways cause the subordinate to feel somewhat dissatisfied with himself in some way—thus the urge to change or develop.

The simplest way to create this gap in the employee's mind is by **leveling**—by telling him or her forthrightly that he needs to improve a specific skill.

You can add some urgency to your message by saying that the employee's job might depend on increasing the skill in question. At that point you enter the realm of discipline, for firing someone is the ultimate punishment. There are lesser punishments of various kinds—no raise, or a poor raise, no promotion, reduced privileges—which you can use to create, in the employee's mind, the urge to develop. There are times that discipline for this purpose is appropriate. However, the use of discipline for fostering self-development is limited in that it creates a false urgency. It is an urgency imposed by you and there is no way to make sure it is deeply felt by the employee. Thus the only way you can make sure it continues is by continuing the threat of punishment for as long as necessary. That requires extraordinary time and attention on your part. There are better ways. Besides, using discipline consistently, instead of as a last resort, builds a relationship of fear between you and the subordinate.

Better, surely, is the method of creating a gap by basing it on the employee's personal desire to achieve something—a goal of some kind. Once the employee has developed a desire to reach a goal—win a production prize, gain a promotion, earn praise, assume new responsibility—you then can point out that developing certain skills is critical to accomplishing that end.

For example, there was the executive secretary who had refused to use a word processor, until she discovered that she could not handle some of her boss's new correspondence (a crucial part of her job, in her mind) unless she used the processor. Her goal obviously was to maintain that special relationship with the boss as executive secretary. When the boss took on responsibilities which required using the word processor, it became difficult for her to maintain that relationship unless she learned a new skill she had not wanted to learn.

Of course, the need for development may be a natural by-product of a more formal goal-setting and planning process, too—such as the Fundamental Cycle. The development of a detailed action plan may make clear that the successful accomplishment of the plan will require some skills not now possessed. The solution is to build into the plan some way to obtain these skills.

Finally, there is one other key technique of fostering a desire for self-development: place the subordinate in a work group where the group work standards create the gap and thus the desire for change. If the regular members of that group possess certain skills and expect that all members will possess them, making someone a new group member will foster that person's need to develop those skills, too. Usually, such a work group will allow the new member a certain grace period in which to learn the skills.

Is the Development of People Consciously Pursued in Chosen Directions?

The key words in this question are "consciously" and "chosen." The point of the question is to determine if the directions in which your people are developing have been carefully selected and intelligently thought out.

It is the rare person in any situation who is not developing in some way. The question is whether the ways are those which you and the employee might want, given the requirements of the work.

If the need and desire for development have been created by the discovery of a gap between the employee's actual and desired skills, then have you and the employee done an analysis of what skills need to be developed and how they best can be developed? That is the point.

It is easy to make too much of this. If there is one skill involved, you probably need little analysis to identify and develop it. Too much analysis can be paralyzing.

In addition, "needs analysis" may sound imposing and frightening. It can involve hours of thoughtful analysis for something very complicated—or only a moment of real thought for something simple. But once the need and desire exist for development, have you given any thought to what development should occur and how? If you have not, the development may pursue a course different from the one you might have chosen. The mere need and desire for change does not mean that the right kind of development will occur automatically.

How Are You Actually Helping People Develop Themselves?

For this there are many techniques, which you should use as appropriate for a given person and situation.

Teaching: This includes outright instruction, whether by you or someone else qualified, either on the job or away.

Coaching: This is not formal instruction, but it involves working with a subordinate on the job—to explain, show, and give feedback as the subordinate tries something new.

Task-matching: This involves putting the person together with the right task, so that the work itself creates both a need for certain desirable skills and the opportunity to practice those skills in the normal course of work. If it is desirable for an employee to understand and analyze budgets, for example, you may want to give that person the opportunity to prepare some budgets as part of his or her regular work. The point is that most skills are developed by using them. Assigning such tasks to an employee may stretch his or her capabilities—that is the point. But be sure there is a high probability of success. If appropriate, team the employee with another employee who has more experience and can help the inexperienced employee learn more quickly, while avoiding mistakes.

Developmental assignments: These are specific and special assignments given (usually in addition to the regular job) because they require the employee to develop or practice the skills he wishes to develop. This is a particularly useful technique when the employee wishes to develop skills for future use. It is basically a means of getting ready for the future—either a new job or an expanded job.

20 Methods of Motivation

One of the functions (and perennial problems) of management is to motivate employees. You might find useful a list of the various major ways to motivate. The list is hardly exhaustive but it should give you some notion of the various techniques you can use.

Praise

Every employee who has worked for a long period has something in his performance worth commending. There must be something work-related that the employee does well, or at least does better than he or she used to. Praise is an obvious form of motivation for most people, and you may sometimes fear it is so obvious it will not work. That is certainly wrong. In every case I suspect that honest, appropriate praise will be gratefully received. I emphasize the words honest and appropriate. Insincere or inappropriate praise is almost instantly seen as manipulation. But a quiet word of commendation, or even a loud one at the right time and place, can make much effort seem worthwhile.

Money

Whether money can truly motivate over a period of time is a controversial subject. There is evidence that it does not motivate over the long term. Yet there is evidence that for some people, perhaps for many people, it is indeed an effective incentive. At least consider it seriously in all its forms: salary, overtime, bonuses, prizes and promotions (which obviously involve more than money). Be sure, though, that they appeal to the person in mind, and be sure that you indeed have control over the granting of the money. In many companies each employee's pay is actually controlled by several people, as well as by company policies and procedures. Where you do not have real control, it would be foolish to use the prospect of money as a primary motivator.

Promotions/Career Advancement

Promotion has been mentioned already, for it usually involves an increase in pay. Yet for many, the honest prospect of an advancement in position (aside from money) is a serious inducement to hard effort and thought. The reasons can be varied. The promotion at stake might be an important step in the employee's career. Or it may simply have great social significance in the employee's personal and community life. Whatever the reason, the prospect of advancement can spur people on. It has limited value, however, for promotions are normally well spaced out in a person's career—years may fall between them. Positions offering an opportunity for advancement may not open very frequently. If the possibility of promotion is at all remote, it can hardly serve to motivate. But if there is a genuine chance that advancement can occur, use that chance as a motivator.

Matching the Employee and the Job

Every individual employee's needs are different, and the capacity of every job to fill needs is different, too. You need to ask yourself if there is a sufficient marriage between the specific employee and the ability of the job to fill that persons's needs. For example, if the employee has a strong need to control his or her own pace of work, yet his job requires him to respond continually to the demands of others, he is not likely to be very happy or motivated; he certainly is not likely to do his best. If there is a problem with the match between the job and person, it can be difficult to change. Better to make sure a match exists when the job is filled, rather than later. If you discover the problem later, it will probably be easier to change the job itself (difficult as that may be) than to change the person.

Are Expectations Clear?

There is much evidence that people react strongly to what is expected of them. If you expect only a certain quantity of work or level of quality, that is probably what you will get. Rarely will someone give you more. That will happen, but you can hardly count on it. So the question is: Have you made clear to the employee exactly what you expect? This will apply not only to specific job measures but also to general performance. There is the famous study done in which teachers were told they were teaching a class of gifted students. This class at the end of the course tested as would be expected of a class of gifted students. But the students had not actually started out as gifted. They were average students and those running the study had deliberately misled the teachers—who had taught the whole course under the assumption that the students were bright. There are similar episodes in business. People tend to perform up to expectations, if they know what those expectations are.

Is There a Match between Responsibilities and Capabilities?

Clearly no one can do well in a job that requires strengths where one has weaknesses. Even highly talented people have weaknesses; it is guaranteed failure to give them duties and responsibilities which require the extensive use of those weaknesses. Change the responsibilities or run the risk of losing the person, either because he becomes disgusted and leaves, or because the sense of failure begins to permeate all his work.

Involve the Person in Planning

Besides all its other benefits, planning is a motivating activity. There is something in carefully thinking out the future and what you will do to accomplish a goal that increases your desire to accomplish the goal. Perhaps doing the planning makes the goal more concrete and real, and planning for its accomplishment makes it seem possible, even inevitable. Whatever the reason, one seldom sees people more eager to work than just after they have finished planning. So, encourage planning and make sure the people who will need to work hard on some activity have been involved in planning it.

Make a Change

The conventional wisdom is that people resist change. That is not necessarily true. Those who are comfortable in their current work situation are likely to resist change. But that is not true of those who are unhappy with their current circumstances, or who are new and have not had a chance to become comfortable. Depending on the nature of the specific change, you may find that such people are in favor of change in principle. The change can be almost anything of importance in the work environment: the office layout, the relationships of workers, the workflow, the assignment of duties, deadlines, and so on. For new or unsatisfied employees, the right kind of change can motivate.

Make the Job Itself Motivating

The way a job is structured can have a large impact on whether the person performing it will be motivated, apart from all the other motivational variables I have already mentioned. The key consideration here is whether or not the job is "whole." Is it a logical, complete chunk of work with an end-product which the employee can identify and look at with pride? Assembly-line work in which each employee performs some trivial task is the opposite of this kind of work. If the job is not whole, it is not likely that anyone doing it will be able to take great pride in it. Does the work produce something which the worker can point to and say with satisfaction, "I did that. It's mine"?

Forthright Appraisals Built around Goals

There is a great deal of evidence that people work harder when they work toward goals. In fact that is apparently so even if the goals are given to them. Even more effective can be goals which people have set for themselves, or have helped to set. Yet the effectiveness of goals depends on forthright feedback—information about how the person is doing in making progress toward the goal. If an employee begins to work towards a goal with great enthusiasm, that enthusiasm is likely to flag unless he can see that his efforts are taking him in the direction he wants. Preferable is a goal which the employee can measure himself. In that case, it is your task as manager to make sure the employee has the necessary information for self-appraisal. In many cases, self-appraisal will not be possible and feedback will depend, at least in part, on you. You will need periodically to tell the employee your judgment about his or her progress. But whatever it is, there must be some way of monitoring progress.

Training

Here we mean almost any kind of training, so long as it is recognized as training by the employees concerned. Training can increase an employee's sense of ability and sufficiency—his or her feeling of "I can do that!" Where there is this sense of ability, there is more likely to be a willingness to use that ability. The opposite is true, too: where the employee feels unable, he or she is more likely to feel unwilling. That is so, even where the employee's feeling of inability is wrong or exaggerated. In that case, you will need to overcome the employee's feeling, either through persuasion or the assignment of simple tasks to show the employee what he can do.

Consider whether you use all these motivational tools. Individual circumstances will dictate which is right for a given employee. But if, over a period of time and several employees, you have not used all or most of them, you probably are limiting your own effectiveness.

21 Work That Motivates

In reading about the motivation of people at work I became familiar with the movement known as "job enrichment." Without suggesting that anyone join that movement or initiate formal enrichment programs, I want to present the key ideas of job enrichment here. I believe many of those ideas are highly and easily usable by the practical manager.

Psychologists identify two kinds of motivation related to work: intrinsic and extrinsic. Extrinsic motivation is that motivation which comes from rewards and other elements added to the work—that is, extrinsic to or outside of the actual doing of the work itself. These include money, title, promotions, formal recognition. Intrinsic motivation is motivation that comes from the work itself and the positive internal feelings that the worker develops from doing the work well.

A few years ago a study of people at work looked at the way work itself was designed. The impetus was a growing concern about the effect on employees of specialization at work—lack of interest, lack of motivation, alienation. One result of this research is what is usually called work or job enrichment.

In general, enriched work is work that has been designed to contain those elements which can motivate people to work harder and more effectively—those elements which encourage intrinsic motivation.

What Makes Work Motivating?

The success of job enrichment led to research that helped isolate those characteristics in a job which determine whether the job is intrinsically motivating or not. Indeed, three aspects of a job seem to determine whether it will be intrinsically motivating:

1. The work must be perceived as worthwhile by the employee.
2. The work must be set up so the employee feels personally responsible for results.
3. The job must allow the employee to determine for himself regularly whether his work is satisfactory.

By these standards the typical assembly-line job will not be very motivating. Inserting and tightening the same set of bolts all day long, for example, is usually not perceived as very worthwhile or important by itself. The employee who performs such a sub-sub-sub-task in the overall assembly of a product probably will find it hard to feel personally accountable for the product. The worker in this case may have immediate knowledge of results or he may not. Certainly, he has little knowledge of how the whole product is coming out.

Work That Motivates

How can you make certain that a given job possesses these three features—meaningfulness, a sense of responsibility, and knowledge of results? An employee, the research found, will tend to feel his work is worthwhile and meaningful if

. . . the job **challenges** the worker's skills.
. . . the job is made of a **whole and identifiable piece of work** with which the employee can personally identify.
. . . the job has a perceivable and personal **impact** on the lives and work of other people.

For an employee to feel a personal sense of responsibility, he must have autonomy—freedom of action, discretion in carrying out work (e.g., in scheduling it), freedom to obtain resources within prescribed limits, and so on. This freedom of autonomy must be sufficient for the employee to feel the success of the work depends on his own efforts and initiative.

This sense of responsibility will also depend on how clearly the job and its responsibilities and objectives are defined.

Finally, to make certain there is knowledge of results, some method of feedback must be built into the job itself so the employee, as he works, can determine for himself the quality of his work. These methods of feedback must be set up in a way that the employee, if the work is unsatisfactory, has an opportunity himself to correct whatever is wrong.

By evaluating a job to see if it has all these characteristics, you can determine the overall motivating potential of that job.

Assessing the Motivating Potential of a Job

When we think of motivation, most of us probably think of people and not jobs. Someone, the employee, is either "motivated" or not. But the concepts of job enrichment force us to look at the job itself. These concepts do not say a person's motivation or drive is irrelevant, but you can hardly expect someone to be "motivated" in a job that is inherently unmotivating.

Following is a list of questions to help you assess the motivating potential of a job (as opposed to the motivation of a person):

1. Does the job challenge the skills of the person in it, and does it require the use of more than one or two simple skills?

2. Does the job involve performing a complete task with which the employee can identify and feel, "This is my territory. This is what I do"? Does the job involve producing a whole product, tangible or intangible, which the employee can call his or her "own"?

3. Does the job involve activities and results which have a substantial impact on other people? Do a number of people other than the person holding the job consider the job important?

4. How much freedom does the employee have—to set his own work schedule, to deal directly with those for whom the work is being done, to spend money within a pre-agreed budget, to deal with problems as he sees fit within the defined scope of the job?

5. How clear are the responsibilities of the job and the relationships built around it?

6. Does the employee get sufficient information about results directly (not through you, the manager), in order to correct any problems or unsatisfactory work?

If you can ascertain for a job that the answers to these questions will be generally positive, then that job has high potential to motivate the employee holding it. If your answers are generally negative, then there is room to make the job more motivating by enriching it.

An Example

Consider one example of an actual enrichment project. The job involved was that of the laboratory technicians whose responsibility was to implement experiments devised by scientists. The technicians set up the necessary laboratory equipment, recorded data and were in charge of the lab assistants. Typically, the scientists refused to delegate anything but routine work to the technicians.

The technicians' jobs were redesigned and enriched in three ways: the technicians were encouraged to personally write and sign the final research report on each project. These reports were issued along with the scientist's reports. Whether the technician's report was checked before publication by the scientist in charge was up to the technician. The technician, however, was fully responsible for his report and had to answer any questions or problems arising from it. Technicians were also more involved in planning the experiments and setting research goals. They were given time (upon request) to pursue their own research ideas; they had to write reports on the results of such projects. They were authorized to requisition materials and equipment within a project budget and to order various kinds of services on their own signature. Also, senior technicians became responsible for training junior technicians, and for interviewing candidates for lab assistant jobs.

Clearly, the technician's job was substantially enriched in a way that increased the technician's responsibilities. As a result, the technician was more likely to feel personally accountable for his work. In addition, the technicians were able to measure their own performances through such means as variances from project budgets, reactions to their written reports, and achievement of project goals.

The results were positive, as measured by the quality and quantity of work produced following enrichment. Similar studies with a wide variety of workers, at all levels, have shown similar results.

22 Steps for Enrichment

This is a sequel to the previous chapter which provided some background on job enrichment. That chapter ought to be read first.

Even the staunchest proponent of enrichment does not claim it works for everyone, or every job. First, not every job needs to be enriched. Second, many jobs by themselves cannot be enriched without changing all the related, surrounding jobs, too. Third, technical requirements may prevent or constrain enrichment.

More importantly, enrichment is not necessarily desired by every employee. When an enrichment program is implemented, enriched work should be made available to everyone in the job category being enriched, but it will not be used by everyone. Some employees will choose to continue as though their work had not changed at all. Why? Enrichment apparently works primarily for those with a high need for growth, development, and learning. Those without this need probably will not be attracted to enriched work. Enrichment will not have a negative effect on those people; it simply will have no effect.

Determining If Enrichment Will Work

Clearly then, before you try to enrich a job, you must determine if enrichment will have any effect. Does the job need to be enriched?

Here are a series of steps for determining if enrichment is worth doing for a specific job:

1. Determine first if the problem in this job really involves motivation and employee satisfaction. Not all problems do. The real problem may be

poor equipment, poor training, poor design of work flow, not enough help—any number of things besides motivation. Work on the real problem—and realize that it may not be motivation.

2. If the real problem *is* one of motivation, then you must determine if it is the job itself which is low in potential to motivate. Or, is the problem the person holding the job? Do not simply assume that it is one or the other. The list of questions presented in the previous chapter can help you determine if the job can be made more motivating.

Note: If you determine that the motivation of the person is low, but the job is potentially motivating, enriching the job will not solve the problem. That is, if the person is the problem, changing the job will not help. However, try to avoid reaching this conclusion too quickly. There are too many cases of "poor" workers who suddenly blossomed after their work was enriched.

3. If motivation in the job is the problem, and the job is low in motivating potential, then look at the specific parts of the job that may be causing the problem. Again, return to the questions in the previous chapter, and look in detail at the answers to each one for the job in question. (Be sure to develop the answers based on hard data in addition to your own opinions.) The answers to individual questions can help reveal which specific parts of the job may be causing the problems.

4. Though the job itself may be a strong candidate for enrichment, you must also ask whether the employee in the job is ready for enrichment. Key question: Does the employee have a need to grow and develop? If not, enriching this job may not have any effect on this particular employee.

How to Enrich

Once you have decided to enrich a job, here are the basic steps and concepts:

1. Redesign the job so it involves a whole, natural piece of work, with a beginning and end, and an identifiable end-product which the employee can point to. Do this by first identifying the basic tasks that comprise the job; then, group those tasks into natural, whole categories. In general, this step will lead to larger modules of work in the job.

2. Set up the job so that the employee can deal with the job "client"— that is, the person for whom the "product" of this job is produced. Someone takes what comes out of the job and does something with it—buys it, builds something with it, sells it, and so on. That person is the client. Set up a direct relationship between the employee and the client—face-to-face, if possible, or on the phone, or by some other means.

3. Design the job so it involves not only doing the job, but also planning and controlling it. This is the most crucial element. For example, give the employee freedom to set schedules, additional authority to request services and items, to spend money within a budget, freedom to set and use time,

freedom to solve his or her own problems. It does no good to give someone a whole job without also giving the authority and control to actually run the job. Otherwise, you have simply made the job bigger but not different or better; the employee will not feel any more responsible.

4. Finally, make sure the employee is able to track his or her own performance—to determine for himself whether he is doing satisfactory work according to standards you and he have agreed upon. This feedback should not come through you or any other manager. It should come directly from the work, if possible. If quality control (QC) is involved, either make the worker responsible for his own QC, or place QC physically close to the worker so he can deal directly with QC people.

Certainly, none of this will make you or me an expert on enrichment, or able to lead a large enrichment campaign within an organization. But the concepts, principles, and guidelines of enrichment are extremely useful for dealing with individual subordinates and trying to improve their work.

Final Comments

Enriching a job is not a replacement for poor salary, poor working conditions, or poor management. If any of these conditions exist, enriching a job is not likely to have much effect. Enriching seems to work best with jobs and groups of jobs where performance has been mediocre but not disastrous, where there is room for improvement, but where there are no fundamental problems.

Those involved in enriching jobs often feel initially that there is great risk in giving too much autonomy to subordinates. Such fears have been groundless when enrichment was properly done. Enrichment is really an opportunity, not a mandate, for individual workers. Poor workers simply do not take the opportunity to expand their work. They do not use the increased freedom. For example, they will continue to ask management to check their work through every step.

One clear lesson of the research into enrichment is that it drastically changes the manager's job. As a matter of fact, it probably forces the manager to **manage** more. When enrichment works properly, it removes from the manager the task of continually checking the daily work of subordinates. The manager no longer spends all day putting out fires for subordinates. Instead, he or she spends the most time on such activities as planning, training of employees, evaluating overall performance, and finding ways to improve the work.

23 Leveling with Subordinates

Being candid, giving negative feedback, criticizing, leveling—there are several words for it, but it always boils down to this: saying something critical to someone. As managers, we may sometimes feel compelled to criticize a subordinate. We are ultimately responsible for that person's performance and sometimes candidness is appropriate.

Perhaps you have a subordinate who is driving you crazy with some fault—he (or she) talks too much (or too little) … he is overbearing (or too self-effacing) … he is not properly respectful (or too unctuous) around superiors … his dress is a little too sloppy. These things are not outright job failures, but in some cases they may affect, directly or indirectly, the person's ultimate job performance, or the performance of others.

You may have avoided confronting the problem altogether, or found some way to gloss over it inoffensively. There is something in many of us which makes us shrink from criticizing someone else formally. Perhaps we realize that we are vulnerable to criticism, too, and that none of us is perfect.

The opposite approach can be a problem, too. Being overly candid too often can make a person hypersensitive, unable to accept useful and constructive criticism.

The word ''leveling'' describes what is really needed here. If the matter at issue does indeed affect the employee's performance (or the performance of co-workers), then it is our job as managers to level with the employee—to have a frank talk with him or her about the problem.

What follows are some ideas to consider in leveling with subordinates.

Manager/Subordinate

As manager, you have considerable freedom to be candid without suffering the obvious drawbacks. You speak and the subordinate listens, you hope; at least he or she probably cannot speak back in the same way. Thus, there is the possibility of abusing your position as manager, even without meaning to. Much abuse probably occurs under the guise of "managing." Always bear in mind that your subordinate is vulnerable to you, as you are vulnerable to your boss.

The result of abusing this vulnerability is that you will lose the subordinate mentally; you will no longer have the ability to influence, lead, and motivate him or her effectively.

Before You Speak

When you feel the need to say something critical to a subordinate—to level—there are some questions you might want to stop and ask yourself first.

Is the problem really related to the job? You are as human as anyone else and your gripes can be as trivial as anyone else's. Be sure before you speak to the subordinate that what you are speaking about is really related to the job. If the problem is only something that bothers you personally, you might be best advised to bite your tongue. If it is not job related, and you do talk about it, the act of talking about it will make it job related. In the process of relieving your feelings you will suddenly have complicated your relationship with this employee immensely. Managing is hard enough without dragging bothersome, extraneous matters into it.

What is my purpose in talking about it? Once you have convinced yourself the matter is related to the job, you still must be even more candid with yourself. Is it your honest intent to improve this person's work? Or, is your real purpose to make yourself feel better? What are your real motives? In case of doubt, keep quiet.

Is the information useful? Your desire to be candid may get this far and still fail the test of "usefulnesss," which can be summed up in a story about Winston Churchill.

Churchill had had too much to drink at some social function when a prominent and candid woman told him, "You are drunk."

"You are ugly," he replied.

"You are still drunk," she retorted.

"Yes, Madam, but tomorrow I shall be sober."

Apparently true, this story illustrates a situation in which two people are leveling with each other. Its humor springs from the fact that the woman was giving Churchill useful information, while his information to her was useless. Drunkenness can be overcome by abstinence, but ugliness is intractable.

Be sure the information you are going to give can be used by the subordinate to improve his or her performance. Deeply ingrained personality traits (e.g., shyness) may be impossible for a person to change.

Am I overreacting in what I think? If you still decide to go ahead, you may find yourself expressing to the subordinate a point of view that you alone hold. If you think someone is overbearing, you probably should test this opinion discreetly, by asking other managers about it whom you trust, before voicing it to the subordinate. Your opinion obviously counts for something, but first be sure that you are not overreacting.

Making the Criticism

You have examined what is on your mind and have decided in good faith to go ahead. Here are some guidelines that may be useful:

• Choose the right time, when the subordinate is best able to handle and learn from what you will say. For example, the middle of a project crisis would be the wrong time. If the criticism is about something that irritates you, do not choose a time when you are actually irritated. The discussion should be as calm and dispassionate as possible. In short, plan the discussion carefully—it should not simply happen.

• Choose an appropriate place where you will have a chance to talk out the problem, where you will be free from interruptions. Treat this as a serious moment because the subordinate probably will, even if (to you) the matter is not a critical aspect of the subordinate's job.

• In telling the subordinate what is on your mind, be as concrete and specific as possible. If you feel the subordinate is too overbearing, it is hardly helpful to make that general assertion. You must give at least one and, better yet, two or more specific, recent incidents in which the subordinate behaved in a way that you considered overbearing. Being able to give only one example can make you look ludicrously picky. On the other hand, pulling out a list of 25 incidents can make you look like Captain Flog. Choose some reasonable balance between the two extremes.

•Make every reasonable effort to ensure that the subordinate understands what you are saying. The subordinate's initial reaction is likely to be defensiveness or denial—"I didn't do that!" or "I'm not like that!" In the subordinate's mind, his behavior is probably logical. In a supportive, objective way you must change that logic. What you say is not right simply because you are the manager. Try to help the subordinate see that there are alternative ways of behaving in a given situation. The "What if?" questions can be gentle eye-openers. Remember that if you truly want the subordinate to change, it will only happen if the subordinate personally decides to change. You can only provide the insight or feedback which begins that process.

• There is a fine line between describing what is wrong and evaluating or judging the subordinate. Obviously, if in your opinion there is something wrong enough to be worth talking about, you have already made a judgment. But you will probably get further if you describe the problem, instead of condemning the subordinate first and using the description to support the condemnation.

• There is a limit to the amount of negative information anyone can absorb at one time. People can almost literally turn off—their eyes actually glaze over—after a certain amount of criticism. No matter what is said after that point, the person cannot absorb it. In fact, the only reaction is to become angry if the criticism continues. Thus, only go so far. There is nothing that says you must express everything on your mind all at once. Proceed in very small steps to give the subordinate a chance to establish a history of improving over time.

• Some people take criticism silently and others react loudly. If there is strong disagreement, back off. That is not to say you should change your position. But do not insist that the subordinate accept your point of view. All you can do is make sure he or she understands your point of view and why you hold it. You might even state that. If the subordinate disagrees and further discussion proves pointless, simply suggest that the subordinate be alert in the future; perhaps he or she will discover what you have talked about.

• Your key concern is that the subordinate understand what you are saying. He/she does not have to agree with it, but make sure he grasps your point. One way of doing this is to ask him to tell back to you what he has been hearing, in summary form. You may be surprised at what you hear.

• Try to get the subordinate to offer some reactions, some feelings about what you have said. Agreement, disagreement, anger, relief, anything ... it is obviously important at this point for you to remain calm. You may even find out some things about the employee that you did not know. You may also, for example, find out that the problem you are talking about is really part of a larger problem that you will have to deal with. Be prepared to accept the employee's reaction, whatever it is, and learn from it.

• If the employee agrees with what you are saying, try to get him or her to make an action plan for change. You can provide valuable support and assistance in that change, but the real effort and initiative must come from the employee.

• If the employee disagrees with what you are saying, explicitly or implicitly, try not to let the discussion simply end. Do not argue. Tell the employee you are taking his point of view under consideration, and that both of you should watch his or her behavior closely for a while and then talk again in the future.

24 Appraising Employees

Most of us probably agree with the idea behind appraisals: people should know where they stand. But when it actually comes to appraising someone else, or being appraised, we often develop a sudden reluctance.

Why bother with appraisals? We may not have any choice because our companies require them. Yet, even if we were not required to do it, appraising employees is still a good idea because 1) an appraisal is the only intelligent basis for pay and promotion decisions, 2) people do like to know where they stand, and most important, 3) if used properly, the appraisal can be a key element in a system for developing and motivating employees for better performance. The appraisal is the final step in the Fundamental Cycle. It is what closes the circle on one iteration of the Cycle and lets you go on to the next.

The Purpose of Appraising

The purpose of an appraisal is to improve the future performance of the subordinate. Thus a performance appraisal is a formal discussion between a subordinate and superior about the subordinate's performance, conducted in such a way that it helps improve the performance of the subordinate.

That leaves much unsaid but it does make the points that a performance appraisal is a formal discussion (not a casual conversation), occurs between a superior and subordinate and, ideally, by reviewing past performance, will lead to improved performance in the future.

An Effective Appraisal ...

Is not limited to the past. If the only point of the appraisal is to appraise past performance, research indicates the effect of the appraisal will range from no effect to actually being harmful to the subordinate's performance. If the appraisal is entirely positive, there is little or no effect because praise seems to have little long-term effect on performance; and if the appraisal is strongly negative, the effect can be harmful, because criticism often seems to lead to poorer performance.

Serves only one immediate purpose. Because appraisals typically support salary and promotion decisions, the appraisal interview itself tends to be used to discuss both the subordinate's performance and salary. In an experiment at General Electric, researchers found that the salary discussion dominated the appraisal session. So they held two separate sessions, one stressing salary and the other stressing performance. You may be constrained by your company's policy in this matter, but if you have the choice, try two separate sessions, too.

Is really a coaching/counselling session. If appraisals are to be used to improve performance, research indicates the superior must play the role of a counsellor or coach. Using the appraisal only to pass judgment implies the belief that a subordinate will do better in the future by knowing how the superior judges his or her past performance. It seldom works that way, and if what the superior thinks is entirely negative, it may have an effect opposite to the one intended.

Most Effective Method: Goal-Based Appraisals

There are several different ways to appraise the performance of an employee. You can compare him or her to other employees, or to a hypothetical ideal employee; you can judge the employee by some totally objective standard (e.g., number of gadgets produced per hour); or you can evaluate the employee against specific performance objectives which had been set specifically for him.

The study at GE found that

... An annual review is too infrequent to have much value for real development.

... Criticism does not usually lead to improved performance.

... Goal-setting, combined with day-to-day coaching on those goals, did consistently improve performance.

The goal-setting method of appraisal, then, is the method of choice where the overall purpose is to improve performance. That is why it is built into the Fundamental Cycle. Each Cycle is closed with a review and appraisal which are the basis for performance in the next Cycle.

The Appraisal Interview

You may find helpful the following guidelines for the appraisal interview itself.

Prepare yourself by reviewing beforehand the subordinate's goals and the performance against those goals. That comparison should be the heart of your discussion.

Begin the interview by **clearly stating the purpose** for meeting. You want the subordinate to be at ease but there must be no question about why you are together.

Cut off distractions. Refuse phone calls. Shut the door. Do whatever is necessary to insure an uninterrupted discussion. If it will help, hold the discussion somewhere private away from your office.

During the interview, **avoid criticism**, particularly of personality traits and anything not directly related to work. There is evidence that criticism seldom does any good and, if heavy, can cause performance to deteriorate. The advantage of evaluating performance against goals is that it minimizes the urge to criticize; shortcomings are more obvious and the discussion can be devoted to finding ways to overcome them, not to what they are and whether they even exist.

You are the interviewer and much of the discussion should **involve the subordinate's own evaluation.** Draw the subordinate out. Listen. Summarize as a means of moving the discussion onward. Wait—there is nothing wrong with periods of silence. Allow the subordinate to discuss feelings. Recognize that initial nervousness and even fear on the part of the subordinate in a situation like this is natural.

Do not minimize real disagreement. Recognize it. Make a list if there are more than one or two areas of disagreement. Try to find some way to resolve them. Try to resolve differences but never force resolution. This is not an argument you must win.

Prepare a summary of the appraisal in writing before your meeting. Let the subordinate read it before the meeting. This will give him a chance to prepare, to collect his thoughts.

There should be a summary of the appraisal interview. You can write it, if you wish, so long as the subordinate has a chance to add comments. Or, the subordinate can write the summary and include his or her reactions. In either case, both you and the subordinate should sign the initial appraisal statement and the summary.

Be sure any action plans coming from the appraisal interview are included in the next Cycle's targets and action plans, as appropriate.

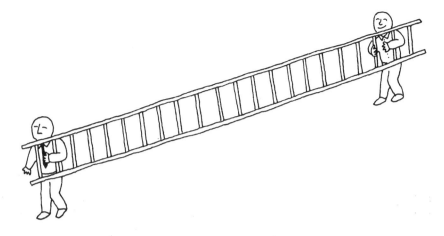

25 Helping a Subordinate's Career Planning

Should we as managers take an interest in the careers of subordinates?

On the one hand, our task as managers is to carry out the objectives and tasks of our assigned areas; the career aspirations of our subordinates have little to do with that directly. Besides, career hopes and plans are private and personal, and none of our business.

On the other hand, we often cannot ignore subordinates' career hopes; we are dealing with whole people, including whatever long-term professional plans they have. In any case, a subordinate is likely to look at his job in light of what it will contribute to his career, so we should be familiar with those plans, to the extent the subordinate is willing to reveal them to us. Finally, there is the argument that, as a means of motivating subordinates, we should be aware of their career plans and consciously try to integrate them into the daily work.

Regardless of this range of opinion there are certain clear points: 1) career plans are personal and we cannot force anyone to divulge or discuss them; 2) however, they play a strong role in the motivation of a subordinate, so it can help if we are aware of them; 3) the proper handling of the question of careers will depend on the subordinate involved—some subordinates will have given no thought to careers, while others will ask us to relate their jobs to their career plans and will even want to discuss their career plans with you. At least we should be prepared when a subordinate raises a career question, and in some instances it may be an appropriate subject for us to raise.

Your Role as Manager

What is the manager's role in this matter of a subordinate's career?

It really comes down to the question of who is responsible for the subordinate's career, and for that matter, for his or her life. Stated this way, the answer to the question is obvious: the subordinate is responsible. It is his/her life, after all. And besides, all development is really self-development.

Given that, here is a definition that I have found useful of the manager's role in a subordinate's career planning: **the only real function of the manager is to help the subordinate take responsibility for his or her own career.**

The manager can do this in two ways: by helping the subordinate plan his (or her) career, and by helping him gain the kind of experience he needs to carry out his plan.

Counselling

Counselling a subordinate about his or her career is not a role that comes automatically with your job as manager. It is something the subordinate must request, or at least allow, you to do. But once the subordinate has asked for your counsel, be clear what that means. It is not the normal managerial role of evaluator, judge, director, leader. Here is what it involves:

Giving information: You probably know more than the subordinate about your organization, about the work he or she wants to do, and so on. You can provide valuable factual information, or you probably know where the subordinate can get it.

Offering professional guidance: If your own career is similar to the one desired by the subordinate, you probably have learned some hard lessons from your own experience that would be useful to someone else coming along. Examples of this might be: what further education to pursue (if any), what professional societies to join, what people to know, what skills to develop, and so on. Of course, your advice is based on your own experience and should be presented as such, but it can be very valuable.

Being a devil's advocate in a positive way: The subordinate's career plans will inevitably be based on various assumptions he or she holds about the career he desires and about himself—his present level of skills, his preferences and dislikes, his ability to develop new skills, and so on. You have observed and managed that subordinate day after day and you can bring a well-founded point of view to an evaluation of those assumptions. For example, the subordinate may believe that he would enjoy certain aspects of a job, when in fact it is those aspects (dealing constantly with strangers, for example) of his present job that he avoids or does least well. You can tell him, ''Wait a minute—you want to do that job, but it involves working a lot with people you don't know. Seems to me that's the part of your job now you dislike most. Isn't that true?''

This may be the most valuable help you can give the subordinate, and you may be the only one who can do it. Again, keep in mind that you are only offering an opinion, and the subordinate is not under any obligation to accept it. Be very careful in offering this kind of advice; it is not an opportunity to make yourself feel good by offering negative opinions. Be prudent in what you say and make sure your own motivation in saying it is truly to help the subordinate.

Helping the subordinate do thorough planning: A career plan is like any other long-term plan. It should contain all the basic elements of a good plan—goal, strategy, actions. While you cannot tell a subordinate what those should be for him, you can remind him that they should be there. In addition, you can make sure he or she has asked and answered all the appropriate questions, such as: What do I really want from my work? Does that jibe with my work experience so far—what I've liked and haven't liked? What skills must I develop to get what I want? What specific skills do I have now? What are the likely steps in the kind of career I want? What does it take to go from one step to the next? How can I use my present job to pursue my career goals?

Remember: your role here is that of a counsellor or coach. You do not control the subordinate's career, nor do you have any final say in any of the basic decisions it involves. It is the subordinate's career and it is his or her career plan.

Helping Subordinates Gain Appropriate Experience

Here is where your helping a subordinate with career plans can pay off in his or her current work for you. Any career plan must begin with the reality of what the subordinate is doing now and how well he or she is doing it. It is equally in your own and your subordinate's interests that the subordinate's career aspirations be integrated into his daily work. It will give special meaning to the work for the employee, and will probably improve the quality of his work.

The first requirement in any career plan is for the subordinate to do well in his or her current job. Moving upward on a career ladder always assumes success at each step. This is obvious but is nonetheless worth pointing out to the subordinate—particularly if he or she is eager to get on with his career but is less eager to pay his dues in necessary, but sometimes unpleasant or unglamorous, work.

Once the subordinate has some idea of his career aspirations, it is possible to review his or her current job in light of them. Tasks that before seemed dull or pointless can take on new significance if mastering them is important to career advancement. Be sure once the basic career planning is done to point this out to the subordinate.

Once you have tied the subordinate's career and current job together, it is possible to build a fruitful and mutually rewarding relationship. The basis of this relationship is that, if the subordinate does his current job well, then you will help with his or her career plan by 1) giving developmental assignments, and 2) helping him move on to the next step when the time is appropriate.

Developmental assignments are projects given to encourage or even force the subordinate to develop in ways and directions that both of you consider useful. These assignments require him to develop new skills, to become acquainted with parts of the organization unknown to him, to deal with new procedures, to get to know people he has not dealt with before, or to assume temporary new responsibilities for himself and for the work of others. The ultimate purpose of such assignments is to prepare him for an expansion of his current job or for movement to a new job. They are not a normal part of any job and are given by you at your discretion.

When the subordinate is ready to move on, you can assist by giving him or her your recommendation, by making other managers in the organization aware of him, or by using your knowledge of the organization (or industry) to help him find a new position.

Of course, the whole idea of career planning means the subordinate will probably leave your work unit some day. There is nothing wrong with that, or with planning it in a way that helps you both.

26 Defining a Job

As managers we are frequently called upon to define formally a job which reports to us. Somehow this requirement often comes at an inauspicious time—such as when we are in a rush to hire someone to fill that position. There is always something better to do. Certainly there are easier things to do.

But easy or not, if we want that new position, or if we want to fundamentally change an existing position, we will need to do that formal job description. Most companies require them, and even if yours does not, the process of defining the job is a useful exercise. Above all, having such a description is a helpful management tool.

The Job Description as a Management Tool

A good job description is accurate, clear, concrete, and complete. Vagueness or inaccuracy will hurt you, either by preventing the job description from being a useful management device, or by creating misunderstandings between you and a subordinate.

How can a job description be used in management? In several ways, I believe, including the following:

• For giving a job candidate a clear and succinct picture of the job he or she is considering. Used in the hiring process, it is almost a "contract" between you and the new-hire as to what will be expected. The better and clearer that description is, the more useful it will be. You cannot expect anyone to take responsibility for something they are not clear about, including their own work.

• As a basic document for setting job goals and conducting performance appraisals with the jobholder. It cannot specify what must be accomplished in a given week, month or year, but it is the starting point for making that determination. It is also a good reference tool for making sure that some basic and important part of the job has not been overlooked in setting performance goals.

• For setting proper and fair salaries, particularly in relation to any other similar jobs.

• For basic management control of the job. Defining the job as suggested in this chapter will almost force you to determine what is most important in it, and therefore what is most critical to watch.

• For helping to define the development needs of the actual person who fills the job. Few people fill a job perfectly. For most of us there is some difference between the way we actually perform a job and the way it should ideally be performed. In order to help someone grow in skill, we must define specifically where that growth needs to occur. That is determined by defining the gap between ideal job performance and the jobholder's actual performance. Yet that gap cannot be defined unless the job itself is fully and clearly defined—and unless the jobholder is aware of, and basically agrees with, that job definition.

If you write a job description and then simply file it away forever, it will serve little purpose. Show it to the jobholder; use it as a reference. If the job changes, change the description. But keep it useful and use it. Writing it is something that seems painful at the moment but will serve you well time after time.

Key Elements of a Job Description

Your company may already have a particular format for job descriptions. You of course should use that. What is presented here is not a specific format but a listing of the key elements an effective job description should contain. Simply make sure that the descriptions you write contain these elements somewhere, regardless of the format. (If you are not required to use a particular format, these elements can be used as one.)

In my experience the key elements in a useful job description are:

• Job title and position in organization
• Reporting relationships
• Job objectives—overall and specific
• Job duties and responsibilities
• Organization relationships
• Requirements for holding the job

The information in these elements essentially should convey what the job is, where it exists in the organization, what activities and responsibilities it encompasses, how performance in it will generally be measured, and what kind of person should hold it.

No job description can or must be all-inclusive. But if it neglects to mention major duties, for example, and it was used in hiring someone, that person will rightfully be able to claim his real job is different from the one he was hired to do. Principally for that reason most job descriptions contain some catch-all language about performing any additional, related but unspecified duties "as required." Including such a clause is fine but no substitute for careful thought about the job.

Writing the Description

The final description is all that matters, of course; any way you choose to get there is fine, so long as you arrive safely. Some managers find it easier to start by making some notes or an outline, beginning with the job objective and then the general duties and responsibilities. Once these are laid out, the remaining elements seem to flow from them.

In any case, what follows is a more detailed description of the kind of information which each of the key elements should contain:

Title and position: This of course is the formal and full title for the position. If this is a new position, you will have to create the title. By "position" I mean the job's location in the organization—division, department, etc. If the job is graded in some way, that should be noted.

Reporting relationships: The position does or will report to some other position (probably yours). That position should be noted as "Reports to:." Also, if the position is managerial or supervisory, other positions will report to it and those should be noted as "Reports to it:."

Job objective: Before describing the details of the job, you should note its overall purpose—the reason or reasons for its existence in the organization. This element should probably not be more than a few lines of writing. Yet it should be specific enough to differentiate the job from others. Note that this is more than a simple description of the job's activities—it is a statement of what the jobholder is generally to accomplish. As noted above, this statement is probably the best place to begin writing the description. You can return and revise it later in your writing, if you wish; but if you begin elsewhere (say, with the detailed duties and responsibilities) you probably will end up confusing yourself and everyone else. Define first the basic job, and then the details will be easier to define clearly.

Duties and responsibilities: In sheer space these will occupy the bulk of the job description. If the job objective is the heart of the job, then these are the muscle. If you wish, divide these into general and specific categories. If the job is managerial, it will include some general management duties. There are various different kinds of duties and responsibilities, and you should cover them all as appropriate, including the following:

1. What is the person in the job responsible for doing, getting done or

overseeing? What are his or her specific activities, including the activities he will oversee?

2. What authority will the jobholder possess? In concrete terms, what will the incumbent be able to approve or authorize by himself?

3. For what things will the incumbent be held finally accountable? If things go bad, what (if anything) will the incumbent be blamed for?

4. How will performance be evaluated—based on what kind of criteria? Performance in any given period will, or should, depend on the specific conditions and goals for that specific period. But it should be possible to describe in comprehensive, though still concrete, terms what will constitute "good," "adequate," or "poor" performance in general.

Organization interaction: Most jobs require that the jobholder interact in some way with other people and groups within the organization, other than those he reports to or which report to him. For many positions, this could be a very long list. It need not be all-inclusive in this description, but it should include those other positions or groups which can have a real effect on the success of the jobholder. This may include people from whom the jobholder gets information, or to whom he feeds information. It may include those whose agreement he must obtain for certain matters. It certainly includes those whose assistance he will require in specific matters. Note the key ones in this section.

Personal requirements: In order to perform the job as you have described it, the jobholder will need to possess certain kinds of experience, training, and personal characteristics. Try to define those here. Be careful not to describe a person who is too rare to find or too good to be true. In the end you must fill the position with a real human being. Defining these requirements thoughtfully will help you find the right person—and it will help the right person find you.

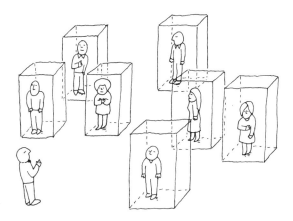

27 The Selection Interview

Before hiring a new employee, we want to make sure there is a good fit between that person and the job. The major way of determining this is by the selection interview, where we have the opportunity to talk to the applicant at length and evaluate him or her in depth. There may be more than one interview with a candidate.

During the selection interview, we can obtain much of the necessary information for assessing the person's skills, pattern of motivation, and ability to grow and develop in the job.

Presented in this chapter is a set of guidelines I developed for conducting a selection interview. The guidelines presume that you are thoroughly familiar with the job to be filled, including the various skills and experience it requires, its potential for motivating different kinds of people, the kind of personality that will work best in it, and to what extent and how quickly it will require growth. Most of all, you must understand what combinations of skills and motives will lead to effective performance in that job. This combination constitutes a rough profile for that job, and the purpose of the selection interview is to find the person whose personal characteristics best match that profile.

Guidelines for the Interview

• Adopt and then follow a general strategy for conducting the interview. Your general choice is between a directed interview and an open-ended interview. In a directed interview you ask a list of predetermined questions which dictate the course of the conversation. In the open-ended interview, you ask key, general questions, but allow the interview to develop as it goes along. The higher the position being filled, the more open-ended your interview will tend to be.

• Experienced interviewers suggest using a checklist, or something similar, as a guide during the interview. A formal list of questions is not necessary, and the interview can still be open-ended with a checklist. The critical thing is that you know what you want to find out, and that you have some kind of guide for making sure you cover everything in the interview.

• Make notes during the interview. They will keep you from becoming hopelessly confused after interviewing three or four applicants. Besides, notetaking is a positive reinforcement for the applicant, a sign that you are listening and consider something he or she said noteworthy.

• A useful way to open an interview is with informal conversation about any areas of common interest you may share with the applicant. Once both of you feel comfortable, you may want to explain what you are doing—describe the job briefly, including the salary range, to make sure it is the job the applicant thinks it is. In general, explain how the job fits into the organization, and what is expected of the person holding the job. Then describe the process you are following to fill the job, including the amount of time you will need to choose an applicant.

• No matter what style you select for conducting the interview, the energy which moves the interview along will come from the questions you ask. So here are some guidelines for asking questions:

... The wording used in a question is important. Do not indicate in the way you ask a question what kind of answer you hope to get. If you telegraph the answer, the applicant is likely to give that answer even if it is not strictly true—that is only human nature. Open-ended questions which cannot be answered with a simple "yes" or "no" are usually more productive.

... It is often useful to restate in question form information you have just received, possibly rephrasing it slightly to check your understanding.

... After asking a question, always wait for an answer, even if that requires a period of tense silence. Try to avoid jumping in with another question or an explanation.

... Silence is an effective tool. When the applicant has answered a question, wait a little bit. He or she may provide more information. Often, this information is much more revealing than any other.

• You often can obtain more useful insights by selecting one situation or case history from the applicant's experience and discussing it in great detail. The alternative is to talk in broad generalities about the applicant's background and experience. That does not give you a true picture of the applicant. If you select a project—any work event with a beginning and an end—and discuss that in detail, you will probably learn a great deal more about the applicant.

• Ask the applicant to describe in detail the project you have selected: What did he (or she) do? How? What did he have to do with other people? Ask about his feelings and reactions at key points. You should remain neutral through this, neither approving or disapproving anything in any way. In fact, your style in this kind of discussion should parallel the way you would work with this person if he or she were a subordinate and you were trying to obtain information. Be yourself.

• During the interview, consider tape recording—not secretly, but with the full knowledge and consent of the applicant. The rationale is simply that the recording is for you alone and it will give you an opportunity to go back and listen to the discussion at a later point. If you record all applicants, it will give you a chance to listen to them all at some later time.

• My own experience and reading have indicated various pitfalls you will want to avoid, because they can lead to poor decisions:

Pitfall 1: The natural tendency is for the interviewer to form an opinion early in the interview and then use the rest of the interview to confirm that opinion. Force yourself to be neutral throughout the interview; you will make a decision later. Try to avoid being too strongly influenced by the applicant's dress or personality or mannerisms. Even the best interview is a high-stress situation, and you probably are not seeing this person as he or she normally appears.

Pitfall 2: If you have several interviews, one after the other, your opinion of an applicant may be unduly influenced by your opinion of those you interviewed immediately before. For example, if you interview a series of weak candidates and an average candidate is next, the average candidate will seem superior in comparison with his or her predecessors.

Pitfall 3: Avoid what is called the "halo effect." This is the tendency we all have to assume that if a candidate is strong (or weak) in one area, then he or she will also be strong (weak) in other areas. We tend to think people are all good or all bad, rather than the mixture of strengths and weaknesses all of us really are.

Pitfall 4: Most interviewers use the interview as a means for **disqualifying** candidates. They find it easier afterwards to describe what was wrong with the candidate than to describe what was right. Everyone, even losing candidates, is usually a combination of strengths and weaknesses. You should hire for strength, not to avoid weakness. Just be sure you know what the weaknesses are and can work around them.

Finally, remember that the interview is a two-way street. You must not only gain information, but also give it. The interview is the applicant's key way of gaining information about you. So, you must both tell and sell—explain the job, sell yourself as a good person to work for, and the organization as a desirable place to work. Encourage questions. Be clear and honest. Be yourself. The way you conduct the interview is the clearest possible indication to the applicant of what you are like as a manager and a person.

Key Points

Know the job and the kind of person most likely to be effective in it—consider both technical skills and motivation.

Use the interview to get information—not to make up your mind. You will make a decision later.

Look for strengths. Be aware of weaknesses, but hire for strength.

Explore with the candidate some specific project from his or her past in great detail. That will give you a much better feel for the candidate than a general discussion.

28 Money and Motivation

Money can clearly be an incentive for some people under certain conditions. A number of studies have confirmed this in general, and your own experience and common sense probably tell you it is true. But the picture is far from clear. Money has been called a "treacherous tool," deceptively easy to use. I know of instances in which money has failed to motivate. The evidence seems to say that money can serve as a powerful motivator but that it is a difficult motivational tool to use. I have summarized here several points which have been useful to me.

Satisfaction with Pay

One must separate the concept of money as a motivational tool into two distinct sets of ideas—money as an incentive and money as a de-motivator. It may not be clear how or when money motivates, but it is clear that a lack of money does de-motivate.

Much of the research on employee satisfaction with pay can be summarized by saying that dissatisfaction with pay can keep people from working their hardest or best, but satisfaction with pay does not necessarily produce the opposite effect. Thus, even if a manager does not wish to use money as a direct incentive, he or she certainly must make sure that employees are at least satisfied with their compensation.

What creates satisfaction with pay? It is not a simple question because some of the elements affecting the answer do not seem to involve money at all.

There is evidence that one can produce satisfaction with pay by grossly overpaying an employee, but that is hardly a desirable solution.

A key element determining satisfaction is that satisfaction often depends on an employee's comparison of his own pay with that of someone else; a favorable comparison helps produce satisfaction, but pay perceived to be low can lead to dissatisfaction.

With whom does an employee compare his or her pay? Often, the comparison group is within the same organization—the same department or division, or people in similar types of jobs elsewhere in the company. However, employees often look outside their immediate organization. An engineer, for example, may compare himself with other engineers in similar jobs in many other organizations. This tendency seems to be related to education; that is, the higher the employee's education and professional standing, the more tendency there will be to look to one's professional group outside than to one's peers within the organization for points of pay comparison.

If there is a difference between what an employee makes and what the average member of his or her pay comparison group makes, how large must the difference be for it to have an effect on the employee's attitude? One study done by the American Compensation Association indicated that differences plus or minus up to 16 percent did not seem to influence the employee's attitude one way or the other. Yet having a salary which was more than 16 percent below the comparison group average was a definite cause of dissatisfaction. Those whose pay was significantly more than the average tended not to be as sensitive to this difference. Perhaps high-paid employees tend to compare themselves with other high-paid employees in their profession, not with their profession as a whole.

If you wish compensation not to be a source of dissatisfaction, consider using the following criteria as guidelines:

• Pay should be equitable—each person paid fairly in relation to his or her experience, performance, and so on.

• Pay should be balanced—a reasonable mix of salary, benefits and other kinds of compensation.

• Pay must be properly administered—according to clear guidelines clearly understood and consistently followed.

There is a paradox here: pay satisfaction does not always depend entirely on pay alone. In some situations, it may not depend on pay at all, in the sense that no realistic pay increase could produce satisfaction. A study was done concerning the preferences of 354 employees in six organizations for the various kinds of rewards, including pay, that their organizations could provide. (Non-pay rewards included such things as good working conditions, job security, opportunity to self-actualize, opportunity to develop in the job, relative autonomy, and opportunities to meet one's need for esteem.) The researchers found that "employees who were satisfied with non-monetary rewards were significantly more satisfied with pay than those who were dissatisfied with non-monetary rewards." "The data strongly suggest," the researchers said, "that managers who are interested in their employees' satisfaction with pay should look beyond salary alone. While monetary rewards play an important role in worker satisfaction, it appears that employees revise their definition of a 'fair wage' on the basis of the total reward system—monetary and non-monetary—provided by their organization."

The results even indicated that there could be a tradeoff between salary and non-monetary rewards, that increasing non-monetary rewards can help remove or alleviate salary dissatisfaction. In fact, the authors suggested that the "greatest improvements in pay satisfaction occur when employees are satisfied with autonomy, closely followed by working conditions, esteem, and self-actualization."

This is not to suggest that you try substituting these non-monetary rewards for fair pay, but you should be aware that unhappiness with pay can be symptomatic of unhappiness with the work itself. What seems to happen is that employees unhappy with their work say (in effect), "You cannot pay me enough to make up for this lousy job." This is not a problem that money can solve.

Money as an Incentive—Merit Pay

Employees who feel grossly overpaid definitely work harder (according to research), apparently in an effort to merit the pay. Yet few companies can afford to overpay employees, and so the question is—how can money be used directly and efficiently to improve performance?

The evidence seems to indicate that, in general, employees like the idea of merit pay plans, if they trust their employer to be fair. Yet actual experience with many merit pay plans is not only that the plans fail to motivate, but that they also have negative consequences. In fact, there is enough negative evidence to cause some industrial psychologists to argue against merit pay plans.

A persuasive case against merit pay plans is made by Herbert H. Meyer. His argument goes roughly as follows: The key problem is that people tend to rate themselves and their performance highly. The average worker usually feels that he or she is above average. (Meyer is talking about a person's private self-rating, which is usually higher than his public self-rating, e.g., in an appraisal interview. Meyer is talking about how a person really feels about himself.)

Unfortunately, the average pay increase under merit pay plans must, by definition, be average. In most cases, the merit pay increase does not reflect the employee's opinion of his own performance. The effect of this on the worker's motivation is likely to be more negative than positive.

In this situation, the manager faces a real dilemma. The effective manager wants to foster in each employee the desire to be an effective performer.

Why? Because functioning well in any aspect of life, including work, requires that one have healthy self-esteem. Few people can function well for long if they view themselves and their work as inadequate.

The effect of the average pay increase, Meyer argues, is to say to most employees, "You're not as good as you think you are." How do people react when their self-esteem is threatened? A few will try to improve. But most, Meyer argues, will react differently. They will press to get job standards lowered, they will downgrade the importance of the job itself, and they will disparage the person (you, the manager) who made or recommended the pay raise. None of these reactions produces a job attitude which fosters effective work.

Meyer's solution is to accept this problem and give up the idea of money as a motivator. So long as the basic pay level is satisfactory to an employee, Meyer feels the manager should try to focus attention on the work itself, not on pay. He cites evidence that when a merit pay plan is installed, employees tend to work for the money and not for satisfaction from the work itself. To the extent pay is related directly to the performance of a task, the employee's intrinsic interest in the task itself will decrease.

However, you may not want to give up the use of money as a motivator. There are situations where it does work. The evidence seems to indicate that for pay to be an effective direct motivator of performance, it must meet these criteria:

• There must be a direct, objective link between pay and the desired performance. The reward and its size should not depend on someone's judgment, but upon attaining objectively-measured goals, e.g., a level of sales, a specific level of costs. The criteria for merit pay must be agreed upon, or at least accepted, by all concerned, not seen as an arbitrary set of standards imposed by management.

• Merit pay plans must be faultlessly administered, promptly and without error.

• Money must be a motivator for those involved. Some people are not motivated by money once their basic needs are met.

• The amount of money offered under a merit plan must be large enough to be considered a true incentive by those in the plan.

• There should be a moderate probability of success for each individual under the plan. Everyone should have a reasonable chance to succeed.

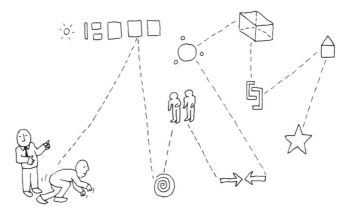

29 A Quick-Start Orientation

Orientation is the introduction of the new employee to his or her new job. The employee may be new to the job, or to the entire organization. In those first few days and weeks the new employee will form impressions about the job and organization which will have a bearing or his or her ultimate satisfaction, competence, and loyalty. Shallow or ill-founded as they often may seem, these early attitudes can be difficult to change because, once they are formed, the employee will look for (and therefore is likely to find) evidence to confirm them.

From our point of view as managers, those early days and weeks are important, for it is then that we need to begin forming an accurate picture of the new employee's strengths and weaknesses. If we have hired carefully, nothing about the new employee should surprise us greatly. Still, we have much to learn about this person, and the orientation period, properly handled, is a good place to begin.

There is some evidence that when a person first takes a new job, he or she is particularly eager to be productive. That makes sense. It is usually the quickest way to be accepted into the average work group—by being useful and doing one's share of the workload. Thus, it would make sense that the quickest and easiest way to get someone motivated at work is to define clearly what his work is—what's expected of him.

Step One—The Initial Interview

You should sit down with the new employee on the first day and discuss the work to be done, as well as the context of the work. In this discussion, you probably will want to cover these points:

• Welcome the new employee. Coming into a new organization is a nervous time for anyone. At this time you might say, in effect, "Welcome! We're glad you are here. The work you are going to do is important to us. We're counting on you, and today I'm going to explain to you how you can make a real contribution to what we do."

• If no one else is going to orient the new employee to the company's basic personnel policies and other fundamental work rules, then you should do so at this point. Ideally, there will be a written document summarizing these items. If not, be sure to review them orally. If this step is normally done by someone else in your company, you might simply ask if the employee has any questions.

• Be sure to explain to the new employee any work rules which are specific to your department or work unit. These may include safety rules, rules about arrival and departure times, lunch and break time, building security, and so on.

• Review the way your department or work unit is organized. Draw a simple organization chart to show the relationships between jobs. Point out the names and titles of key people.

• Explain on that organization chart how the new employee's job fits into the organization, and how the work of that job relates to the work of other jobs, both inside and outside your work unit. Keep this chart, so that later you can refer to it.

• This initial meeting is an opportunity to begin answering key questions which will probably be on the employee's mind. Obviously, the specific questions can vary widely, but you should be prepared to discuss the following:

"**What is my job?** What do you expect from me? What quantity of work must I perform? At what level of quality? How quickly? In my work, must I relate to others? What do these others expect of me? What must I give them, and what must they give me? What kind of help can I expect from them, and you?"

"**How will you (my boss) evaluate my work?** Will there be any formal evaluations? If so, when? On what basis will you make the evaluation? Will I know beforehand the standards by which you will evaluate me?"

"**What are the opportunities for advancement?**" You may not be able to discuss this in detail, and you certainly should avoid anything that even hints of a promise. But it might be appropriate to talk about any other employees who have advanced in the organization, and what paths they followed.

As part of this discussion, you might cover any policies and procedures on salary. Review the specific salary you will be paying this person, as well as the salary range for the job (if there is one). Let the employee know how often the salary will be reviewed and on what basis it will be changed.

In this initial discussion, try to keep everything simple. Provide a simple framework of major points that the employee can use to make sense of the new information he or she will be gathering in the days and weeks ahead.

Step Two—Introductions

Introduce the new employee to other employees. But to avoid a blur of new faces, limit the number of people introduced to as few as possible. As you introduce the new person around, take with you the organization chart you developed at the initial discussion. As you introduce someone, explain where that person fits on the chart.

Step Three—The Initial Assignment

The best way to learn something is to start doing it. So, at the very beginning, unless the job is completely routine, think about giving a specific assignment to the new employee. It does not particularly matter what the assignment is, except it must meet these requirements:

• It must involve necessary work, not obvious make-work. And it must be related in some clear way to the work the employee will be doing permanently.

• The assignment should require interacting in some tension-free way with other key people. That may even include your superiors, if the new employee will be dealing with them as part of the job.

• Be sure that the result of the assignment is nonthreatening. There should be little chance of real failure, and the employee should not be put on the spot right at the beginning. An ideal result might be some type of plan. That will let you review the results—if there are problems with it, there is no real harm done.

• Such an orientation assignment can serve three separate purposes: first, necessary work will get done; second, the new employee will begin to learn the job, be productive, and deal with other employees; third, it will give you a chance to observe the new employee in an actual work situation in which there is little threat of failure. This third benefit is an important one because it will let you begin to get answers to these key questions:

What kind of relationship does this employee want? How does he want to be managed?

What level of skill and knowledge does he or she really possess?

How much time will you have to spend with this person each day?

How well does he or she work with other employees? Will there be differences to smooth over?

Step Four—A Second Discussion

At some point not far off—perhaps when the initial assignment is done—

you should meet a second time with the new employee. Review again in more detail the key questions that you covered briefly in the first discussion. Now, the employee will have the benefit of some actual work experience in the company, and your answers to the questions can have more detail and substance.

30 Managing Turnover

The common wisdom about turnover is that it ought to be avoided. Companies have developed a number of techniques to reduce it: high pay, an emphasis on company loyalty, pension plans that vest over a period of years. These and other techniques are designed to keep turnover as low as possible.

Why? The traditional argument is that the cost of replacement, the disruption to the organization, and the loss of experience and training are so high that turnover should be reduced to a minimum.

But there is another point of view, argued compellingly by Saul Gellerman in an article a few years ago. He said that what we should do with turnover is **manage** it. What he said contained so many worthwhile ideas that even if you do not accept his overall thesis, the ideas may still be useful. Here, in brief, is his argument.

The Advantages of Turnover

Imagine what it would be like if no one ever left your department or organization. You would lose the influx of new ideas, and your organization would become entirely inbred. You would eventually be paying everyone at the top of their pay scales. There would be nowhere for anyone to go, either in pay or position. Opportunities for advancement would arise only when someone died or retired. Ultimately, you would have an organization filled with people who had no place to go, bored with their work, unmotivated.

That is the result when there is no turnover.

Here are the advantages of turnover: fresh ideas, the infusion of new talent, the ability to fill the inevitable dead-end jobs with people who take them to get valuable experience and then move either up or out. Turnover tends to reduce the average experience level of people within a group or organization; thus, the average pay level tends to be at or below the midpoint of salary ranges. This gives the employees enough room for advancement in salary and gives management a means of motivating them by the prospect of increases in pay.

Some Companies Encourage Turnover

Gellerman pointed out that certain companies have a reputation for training employees well. A few years with such a company is recognized as an excellent background. These companies, in fact, encourage turnover. They set very high entrance standards for new employees. Nonetheless, they never lack good applicants because they are known for investing a great deal in training employees and giving them valuable experience. After a few years, these companies will keep only the cream of this already-creamy crop. Thus, everyone benefits. Most employees leave, but they have gained valuable training. The companies benefit because they have obtained, in both the short and long terms, a higher level of employee than they might ordinarily have gotten. Yet, the usual standards of turnover would probably indicate their turnover was too high.

Managing Turnover

Gellerman's comments were aimed at organizations as a whole, but with some intelligent adaptation they can apply to a department or any other work unit as easily as a whole company. Try to think of them in light of the unit you manage.

What does managing turnover mean?

According to Gellerman, it means that you accept turnover in general as a fact of corporate life. You recognize that there are certain benefits of turnover. You recognize that if someone remains in the same job for a long time, that person is likely to become unmotivated. Accept the fact that, as people grow and develop, you may not be able to provide opportunities for continuous growth and challenge. People do reach the limit of what a job or an organization can give them, and the only way they can advance may be by going to another organization. The point of motivating and developing people is not to keep them forever, but to get maximum benefit from them while they are in your organization.

Recognize that some jobs are inevitably dull and lead nowhere. If you fill such jobs with older, experienced people, they will probably atrophy in those positions. By hiring older people you can minimize turnover. (In fact, the quickest, sure-fire way to reduce turnover generally is to hire older people; they are not as likely to leave as less experienced, younger employees.) However, for dead-end jobs you might be better off hiring a succession of younger people. Turn these positions into training positions. Expect high turnover in them and plan for it.

Above all, the key to managing turnover is not to worry about how many people leave an organization, but which people leave. This is based on a simple idea: If we are honest, we will recognize that virtually everyone (including ourselves) is replaceable. Replacing people is an immediate inconvenience, especially if you are unprepared for it, but over the long term, there are few people, even good ones, who simply cannot be replaced.

With that in mind, here are some pointers for pursuing the strategy of paying attention to who leaves, not how many:

• Identify those employees who are absolutely critical to your company. This includes those who are capable of growing to the higher positions or possess rare talents that are absolutely essential to your company's well-being. Be very tough-minded in identifying these people. There will not be many of them, even in a large organization. You can usually identify them by what they have actually done. If they are truly irreplaceable, you probably cannot conceive of anyone else having accomplished what they have.

• Once you have identified these few people, you should take steps to keep them. If necessary, try to overpay them—pay them more than their immediate market value. So far as is possible and fair, treat them as special. You probably will have to work this out with your superiors and your company personnel department.

• If any of these people ever express a desire to leave, try to find out what it is that attracts him or her elsewhere; perhaps you can provide that in your organization. In the end, though, you probably cannot stop someone from leaving if he or she had made up his mind to go. In that case, let the person go—but don't give up. Stay in touch and re-recruit the person at some appropriate time in the future. Have lunch occasionally. Stay aware of how the person is doing in his new company. At the right moment, let him or her know that there is a position available with you if he is every interested.

• If such a person actually leaves, be sure to find out in some detail why he or she is leaving. If there are problems in your organization which are pushing this person out, you will need to solve the problems.

• For the rest of your employees—it is not important to stop them from ever leaving. The critical point is simply to make sure they stay long enough for the organization to gain the benefit of their training and experience. The fact is, Gellerman said, that most employees reach their top productivity in a job within the first few months or years. Once an employee has reached this point of top productivity, additional experience in the job does not provide any real benefit. Thus, you certainly will want an employee to remain in a job beyond the point of becoming fully productive. But once the employee has reached that position, and held it for a reasonable length of time, there is no particular benefit in keeping him or her. Most of all, you cannot want someone to feel stuck in a job, either because he or she is too highly paid to leave, or he has too much invested in the company, or because the company, as a matter of policy, discourages anyone from leaving. The critical element here is to make sure that a person's pay does not exceed his (or her) market value—what he could command in a similar position elsewhere.

• Handle the notion of turnover in the open. Let it be known that you consider it a fact of life. The virtue of this approach is that if someone is planning to leave, he or she will be more likely to let you know in advance. If turnover is officially discouraged, you are likely to find out about it only at the last moment. That will certainly make it more of a problem for you. If employees leave before you have gotten the benefit of their training and experience, then something is wrong; if they leave after that point, you probably should not worry too much about it.

Summing Up

Turnover needs to be managed, not avoided.

Identify those few employees who are irreplaceable and take special steps to keep them, or to bring them back if they should leave.

Beyond that, turnover is a major problem only if people are leaving before you have received any benefit from their training and experience.

Treat turnover openly, as a fact of life. You will be more likely to find out in advance about people who are thinking of leaving, and that will let you plan for their replacement.

31 Employees with Personal Problems

Managing an employee whose work is suffering because of personal problems can present a dilemma. The problems originate away from work, and so are not your business. Yet if they affect the employee's work, you must do something about them.

An example might be an employee with a sick child, or an employee getting a divorce and having to spend time in court or negotiations. The employee whose problem is alcoholism or drug abuse also falls into this category. All of these are real, legitimate problems that could fall on any of us.

Why Bother?

Why should you concern yourself with such things? You are responsible only for the work. All you should have to worry about is whether the work is done or not. If it is not, then you will take steps to make sure that it is. If an employee's work falls and remains below the level of quality or quantity expected, then the employee will ultimately have to leave that job.

Yet asking an employee to divide his or her life into two completely separate categories, life and work, is too much to ask. An employee's life, like your own life, is one whole unit. What happens in one part affects what happens in another. You cannot ignore the effect of the employee's problems, and so you must somehow come to terms with the problems.

The way you handle an employee with personal problems will affect your other employees and their morale. Your willingness to "walk a mile" with employees who have legitimate problems may encourage them to return the favor. You are not likely to get consistent maximum effort from people who feel that you give them only the barest minimum of consideration.

Of course, this works both ways. Employees in general do not usually want to see an individual employee singled out for special treatment—good or bad—unless there is a sound reason.

In some situations you may feel compelled to take personal problems into account because there may be a reason to believe that the personal problems were indirectly caused by your organization—by the pressures of work, the necessity of heavy travel, or late hours, for example.

What it comes down to is that you must deal in some way with the personal problems of the employee, if those problems are hurting the employee's work. You cannot ignore their effects, and if you wish to remove the effects, you must deal with the causes.

The question is, what can you do about them? How can you act in a way that mitigates the effects of the problems, improves the quality of the employee's work, and maintains or even improves the employee's commitment to work?

As this was written, there was little research material on how to handle employees with such personal problems as a child with an extended illness, or a messy separation and divorce, or a dying parent. However, there is informed opinion and information on dealing with employees who are alcoholic or on drugs.

The approach taken here is to cover that information on drinking and to extract from it general guidelines for handling employees with personal problems in general.

One Extreme—Alcoholism

Alcoholism is more common than you might suppose. In a typically large organization, some four to five percent of the employees will have a drinking problem. It can affect an employee's work in many ways, but seldom does it actually involve on-the-job drinking. More often it reveals itself, for example, in chronic tardiness or periodic absences which are unannounced and cannot be explained by any good reasons, medical or otherwise.

The advice of those who have worked with alcoholics is this: the most fundamental, important action a manager can take is to confront the suspected alcoholic. By confrontation, I mean a calm and frank discussion, not a heated yelling match, to make the employee face reality **about his or her performance.** The typical alcoholic will deny that he has a problem. He may admit to some drinking but will deny that it is affecting his life or work. He will manufacture endless excuses.

You must realize that you, the manager, may never have absolute hard proof that this employee has a drinking problem. But you must deal with the evidence—the concrete effects on his work.

In confronting the suspected alcoholic, there is no need to accuse him (or her) of drinking. All that is necessary is to make absolutely clear that his observable behavior (e.g., unexplained absences without notice) is unacceptable and will eventually, but certainly, lead to termination.

You would do well in the case of such an employee to keep good records, not only of the absences (or other unacceptable behavior), but also of your talks with the employee (records of what both of you said). Initially, this record may be entirely informal and off the record; but later, if you need it, you will have it.

Managers typically do not want to confront the suspected alcoholic with his or her behavior and its consequences. They may even try to cover for him. These managers' general line of reasoning is that "So and so would be a good employee, except for his drinking problem." Unfortunately, many people consider this kind of thinking compassionate. In fact, it is simple avoidance. It keeps the problem from being solved. The more helpful and ultimately more compassionate attitude is this: "So and so's work is not acceptable. It could be, if he stopped drinking." The mistaken attitude is only a way of covering for the employee, who will likely encourage you to take it.

Many companies have established programs for helping employees with alcohol or drug problems. Once an employee is identified as possibly having a problem, and is confronted with the effects of the problem on his work, he should be put into the program.

Good programs usually include these steps: an employee who has been referred for an alcohol (or drug) problem to the personnel office should, in turn, be referred to a doctor (selected by the company) for examination. If there is direct evidence of alcoholism, or if the examination clearly indicates alcoholism, the employee should be confronted directly with his or her condition. He should then be given two alternatives: if he does not seek professional help, and starts to drink again, he will be immediately fired as soon as it affects his job. However, if he seeks professional help, and while undergoing professional treatment begins to drink again, he will be treated as though he were sick; that is, he will be placed on sick leave, according to the company's regular sick leave policy. When a doctor certifies that he can work, he may return, just as if he had had an auto accident or heart attack.

If your organization does not have such a program, you should consult the local chapter of Alcoholics Anonymous. It is likely to have information and advice about managing alcoholics, or it can refer you to an organization which does.

General Guidelines

• Once you recognize there is a genuine problem—e.g., an employee has been out or severely late many times for no good reason—you must confront the problem. This does not mean anger and loud words, only that you let the employee know there is a problem and that the two of you must talk it out.

• You should position yourself so that you do not become involved personally in the employee's problem. Let's say an employee is having trouble with his spouse. You can certainly make known your personal concern (assuming you are indeed concerned), but under no circumstances should you become part of the problem. Do not, for instance, call the spouse on behalf of the employee.

• At the same time you express your interest and concern, you should make clear your responsibility as a manager. That is, you are responsible for the work and the work must go on, even though there are personal problems. Otherwise, a lot of other people who work with the person could be hurt. You must position yourself as someone who is concerned, but also responsible.

• Keep records of the incidents, the discussions, and of any verbal agreements you and the employee might make. At first, these records can be purely informal—slips of paper thrown into a file. Some managers routinely keep a log, a large notebook, for recording notes about all aspects of the job, and they simply note the incident or discussion in this log. Small incidents or problems sometimes have a way of eventually becoming big. If they do, you will need that information. Don't trust your memory. Besides, notes made at the time have much more credibility than simple memory.

• It is important that you treat everyone who works for you essentially the same. This does not necessarily mean that you treat everyone the same all the time. You may have arranged with an employee that he or she can come in late for a week because of a personal problem and can make it up some other way. That is fine, but you must be willing to treat all other employees, under the same circumstances, in the same way. Above all, you cannot treat those whom you personally like differently from those you like less or not at all.

• The key to handling a problem is that, as soon as it has been identified and confronted, the employee must begin taking action to overcome the effects of the problem at work. The consequences of the problem on the employee's work must not be allowed to drag on indefinitely. You and the employee should agree on the way the employee is either going to solve the problem, or adjust to it so it no longer affects his or her work.

• In most cases, this will mean that you and the employee should work out some kind of plan, formal or informal, for solving the problem or removing its effects on work. The plan may involve some temporary adjustments by you and the employee. It should include the classic elements or a good plan: a definition of the problem, a time limit, clear action steps, and a definition of the limits beyond which the work cannot be affected.

• What if you and the employee are unable to reach agreement on the problem and on what the employee is going to do about it? Then you must make clear what will happen if the employee's work continues to suffer.

What those consequences are will depend on you and the nature of the problem itself. In an extreme, it will mean the employee must be terminated. Whatever the consequences, make sure the employee understands them. If it has reached the point where you must talk about ultimate consequences, you should state them in writing. Then, if the problem continues beyond the limits you established, you must carry out what you said you would do.

• Be sure to keep your boss informed of the problem and what you are doing about it.

32 Effective Discipline

Discipline, broadly defined, is any management response to the breaking of a work rule. It may or may not involve punishment. Whether it does or not, the purpose of discipline is to prevent the breaking of the same rule in the future.

The way we as managers enforce rules may seem a mundane matter, but the way we handle discipline can have a serious effect on morale. If there is no discipline, there is likely to be no respect for management, and for the rules, and no sense of leadership. On the other hand, there are equally harmful effects if discipline is unfair, capricious or unreasonable.

A survey of personnel departments in many companies of different sizes revealed that most discipline problems revolve around attendance—but discipline can also involve a wide variety of problems, including such gray areas as subtle, but definite, insubordination. And it can affect all levels of a company, from the lower levels (where work rules are more clearly defined), to the middle and upper levels (where the rules that employees live by may often be unwritten).

In any case, we should be aware of how to discipline effectively. It may be necessary for us at times to take disciplinary action. Or, discipline problems poorly handled at lower levels will probably find their way up the organization to us, and we will have to make some judgment about how well they were handled.

Why Don't Managers Discipline?

Managers often fail to discipline employees for many reasons. They may not have the knowledge or skill to discipline effectively. They may be afraid that their disciplinary action will be overruled by higher management. They may feel that the employee who broke the rule is aware of what is wrong and there is no need to do anything. They may feel that the discipline will require more time than it is worth. They may feel that handing out discipline will lose the friendship of the employee involved. They may feel that they themselves might have broken the same rule at times, and will not want to discipline someone for something they have done themselves. Or, the atmosphere in the company may not be the kind that supports discipline.

Confronting the Problem

Where an employee has broken a work rule, it is critical that you (the manager) confront the problem immediately, in a calm but firm way.

That confrontation should take the form of a discussion with the employee, preferably in private. You should point out why the employee's behavior was unacceptable. Then, try to determine the cause of the problem.

This is a critical step, for you must determine the cause if you are to help prevent it from happening again. Get the facts. In this entire discussion with the employee, focus on the problem itself, and the effect it has (or had) on work, including the work of others; try to avoid any outright or implied judgment of the employee as an individual.

The "Hot Stove Rule"

The "hot stove rule" is a graphic and memorable way of summarizing the characteristics of effective discipline. It says essentially that breaking a rule should be like touching a hot stove—that is, the result should be predictable, immediate, impersonal, and consistent.

Predictable: The employee should know beforehand that if he or she touches the stove (breaks a rule) he will be burned (punished).

Immediate: The result should occur right away, not at some later time.

Impersonal: The result should occur because the stove was touched (the rule broken), not because the stove somehow "dislikes" the person touching it. Personal feelings should not be involved.

Consistent: The result should always be the same. If someone touches the stove, he (or she) will always get burned; if someone breaks the rule, he will always be disciplined.

All of these points are key to effective discipline, but if one is most important to the development and motivation of employees, it is probably the need for impersonality. The employee being disciplined should see the discipline as impersonal, that is, not directed at him or her personally by another person. The discipline should be a result of breaking a rule, and it should be directed at the **behavior** of the employee, not the employee as a person.

You must, in every way, avoid the impression that the employee is being disciplined because you are angry or upset. You may be, and it may be obvious that you are. But the discipline should not be seen as coming from you personally, but from the infraction of the rule itself.

Thus, in dealing with the infraction, it is important that you keep attention focused on the infraction, the offense, and not on either your anger or the person who broke the rule. That is, do not deal with the person's character, or attitude, or race, or beliefs. Deal only with the infraction.

The Effects of Poor Discipline

Poor use of discipline will reduce your effectiveness as a manager. If the discipline is unpredictable, it will be seen (and so will you) as unfair and arbitrary. If the discipline is not immediate, it violates the obvious psychological principle that a consequence, to have real effect, must follow immediately upon the cause. The purpose of discipline is to prevent future infractions; if there is no immediate connection between the discipline and the infraction, how can it have any effect on future infractions?

In many companies, there is a "due process" procedure that must be followed before discipline can be administered. In that case, the employee must be immediately informed that he or she is in jeopardy of discipline, though the actual discipline may come later.

If discipline is perceived as something personal, the message it then conveys is this: to survive and do well in your organization, one must establish good personal relationships with management, instead of doing good work and obeying the work rules.

If discipline is inconsistent—that is, if management's reactions to rule infractions are not always the same—then employees are likely to think the rules are a game, the object of which is to break the rules and see if discipline can be avoided. Or, employees will break rules based on their weighing of the odds that they will be caught and disciplined.

Appropriate Discipline

The one attribute of effective discipline which the "hot stove rule" does not express is that discipline should be appropriate. This is the industrial version of the maxim that "punishment should fit the crime." If discipline is inappropriate—too much or too little for the seriousness of the infraction—then it will probably have the same effect as if it were unpredictable: it will be seen as unfair and arbitrary, and will likely create an atmosphere of resentment between the employees and the managers.

Make Sure People Know the Rules

You cannot fairly or effectively punish someone for a rule which does not exist, or which has never been thoroughly communicated to all employees. Nor can you discipline someone in a way that has not been made clear beforehand. That is, the rules, and the consequences of breaking the rules, should be communicated clearly to everyone involved far in advance.

Such communication should be a part of the normal introduction and orientation of new employees. Where appropriate, the rules should be put into writing. If you expect everyone to wear a suit and tie and white shirt, tell them that. Ideally, you should tell them that before you hire them, so they can decide whether they want to work under the rule or not.

All of what is said in this chapter is based on the assumption that the rules have been relatively well-defined and communicated clearly, as have the consequences of breaking them. It also assumes that the work rules are reasonable. Insisting on rigid adherence to the rules, in a situation where the rules are not necessarily applicable, may not be appropriate. If you find yourself in a situation where the rules seem to you inappropriate, talk to your boss.

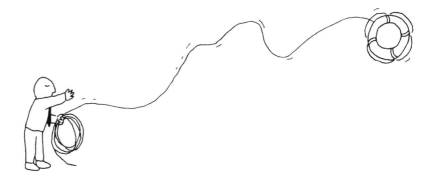

33 Salvaging the Marginal Performer

All of us as managers must deal at some point with an employee whose work is simply not quite good enough. This employee's work is not so poor it merits outright firing, and at times it may be completely acceptable. But overall, his or her performance is right on the line between satisfactory and unsatisfactory.

The clear and obvious choice is either to improve—salvage—the employee to the point that his (or her) work is satisfactory, or remove him from your work unit. In practice, that is not such an easy choice to implement.

Deciding What to Do

Suppose you have decided that a given employee's performance is marginal. That is, his or her work is neither fully acceptable nor fully unacceptable. In reaching that decision, you have probably also decided that the employee cannot continue at that level; the work must improve, or else the worker must be terminated.

Consider Your Alternatives

To ''terminate'' here means simply to remove someone from a specific position. It does not necessarily mean that the person is separated entirely from the organization. The person can be demoted, promoted (not likely, but theoretically possible, depending on the person's previous record), transferred, or, in some cases, offered retirement. If your decision is not to salvage the employee, then you should consider all these alternatives. The right choice obviously depends on the person involved, the circumstances, and the organization.

Salvage or Terminate?

Here is a checklist of items to consider when thinking about a specific marginal employee, and making the decision to salvage or terminate. The relative merits of each element will vary case by case.

Consider the employee's **performance record**. Has there been any improvement at all? Has the performance deteriorated? Has the employee shown any evidence of beginning to improve, or being able to improve? In short, is there any evidence the employee can do better? And, has the employee had a real opportunity to do better?

Consider the employee's **length of service**. If the employee has been with the organization only a short time, you may conclude that there is a simple, obvious mismatch, which is better rectified now than later. However, if the employee has been with the organization a long time, then all concerned must wonder why marginal performance has been accepted for so long. Even if you do not consider length of service an important factor, other employees probably do. Be aware of the possibility that, by terminating such an employee, you may create ill-feelings among other employees that you will have to deal with in the future.

Consider the **skills involved**. Consider whether or not the skills possessed by this person are in short supply. Will you have difficulty finding a replacement? Or will that be relatively easy? If it will be difficult, that is a strong argument for trying to salvage. If it will not be difficult, then the skills involved are not a factor one way or another.

Consider the **difficulty of the job**. Recognize that there are impossible, "killer" jobs which consume the people in them. Does this job have a history of high turnover? Have several people held it in the recent past? If there is someone you know and trust who has held it before, you might be able to discuss your problem with that person confidentially to get another point of view. If these or any other signals exist which indicate the problem may be with the job itself, then you should look at the job first, instead of the person.

Consider the employee's **apparent motivation**. In general, would you consider this employee motivated and willing to work? Or is motivation a problem? Again, if motivation is involved, you must look at both the person and the job. Has this employee performed another job successfully before taking this job? If so, you might talk to the employee's former supervisor. Are there any indications that the employee is working hard? A simple, but effective, method here is to try looking at the job through the eyes of the employee. Put yourself in his or her shoes.

Consider the **quality of management**. In making the salvage/terminate decision, you must always look at the quality of management which you, the manager, have given this person. You may simply not have had the time to work with the person. Your expectations may be unfair or unreasonable. The job may not be clearly defined. There may be problems beyond the employee's control which only you can handle. If there have been management problems, you must ask whether they will be remedied. If not, you realistically may need to find someone who can perform in spite of them.

Consider the **investment in the employee.** If the employee has gone through a lengthy training and orientation period, and the organization has put considerable money into his or her preparation, you may be loathe to let the person go. On the other hand, there is no point in continuing to invest in someone who is not working out, and does not show signs of being able to improve.

Think about **personal considerations.** Is this individual doing badly because of a social mismatch between you, or other workers, and him (or her)? If that is the case, there may not be anything you can do about it, so you should move the employee out of this position as quickly and humanely as possible. A few changes in simple work assignments or work rules, however, can sometimes change everything.

Consider **the effect of the employee's performance on other employees.** Allowing one employee to get away with substandard work can reduce the morale and motivation of other employees. On the other hand, not giving someone a fair chance can also have a bad effect. If you were to terminate this employee, without attempting a salvage, how do you think it would be viewed by other employees?

Is the employee aware that his or her performance is at least partially unsatisfactory? Have you told him so clearly and unequivocally? Do not make any assumptions here. You can hardly terminate someone without telling him first that his job is in jeopardy and giving him, in effect, a probation period for improving.

In making your decision, you might list all these elements, as well as any others that may be important in your specific situation, and give them relative weights. Some of them may not count at all in a particular case, and others may be critically important.

Or, you may classify the elements into three categories: very important, important, not important. Then, use the same categories to group your answers. If most of your "very important" answers indicate salvage, that is probably the answer, even if many of your remaining answers indicate termination.

Working with the Marginal Employee

The first step is to counsel the employee about the poor quality of his or her work. Here are some basic guidelines for doing that:
- Remember the basic principle that all improvement is ultimately self-

improvement; the marginal employee will improve only if he recognizes that his work is marginal and that he should improve. He will not take this attitude simply because you tell him his work is unsatisfactory.

- Helping the employee see the necessity for self-improvement may require lengthy discussions. To participate effectively in these discussions, you must be very familiar with the employee's work and the particular problems he or she faces. You must talk in very concrete terms with the employee about the way he works and the way he might be able to work better.

- Your discussion with the employee should center around what are often called "critical incidents." These are specific situations and events from the employee's own job which you can use to illustrate what you believe is right and wrong with the employee's work. Your discussion with the employee will be far more fruitful if it centers around such specific case histories, than if it concentrates on personality traits and general management principles.

Above all, you cannot "tell" the employee what is wrong. You must counsel him. This requires not only knowledge on your part, but also patience and time. Your ability (or even willingness) to invest this time may be a factor in your original decision to terminate, as opposed to salvage.

- If the employee does not or cannot come to recognize that he (or she) faces a severe problem, then ultimately you must put him on notice. You must say, in effect, "Your work is not satisfactory because of these reasons: (give the reasons). I believe you can correct the problems, but you must determine that for yourself. In any case, if your work does not improve, and meet the minimum standards for the job, then you will have to leave the job." Then, you must describe what concrete standards you will use to judge the employee's performance in the future.

- Once the employee has recognized the need to improve, he or she must develop a plan for improvement. This is a plan for lifting work performance to acceptable standards. You must define the standards for, or with, the employee, but he must define what he is going to do to reach those standards. It must be the employee's plan. And, formal or informal, it should have all the classic elements of a plan—a goal, a deadline, a series of action steps to be taken, sources of help (including you), and a list of obstacles to be overcome and ways to overcome them. If you must develop this plan for the employee, it is not as likely to be followed. You can help the employee develop the plan by providing information and by asking probing questions, but your role must be to assist, not to "do."

34 Firing an Employee

Firing an employee, I think, must be one of the most difficult management tasks of all. There is no way it can be pleasant for anyone concerned. Yet, in some cases it is essential for the good of the organization and perhaps even for the good of the individual being released. Whatever the situation, firing is always the responsibility of the manager.

When Necessary?

A personnel director for one large company, after studying his company's records, noted that 11% of the company's terminations were involuntary—people were fired. He noted, though, that the percentage could have been higher; not everyone was fired who perhaps should have been.

The more common reasons for firing an employee seem to be the following, in no particular order:

- For cause—stealing, drug or alcohol use at work, lying, falsifying records, and so on.
- For a lack of skill—or general inability to do the job.
- For a lack of motivation—or unwillingness to do the job.
- For personality conflicts between an employee and other employees or superiors.
- For flagrant and/or continuous disobedience of reasonable orders.

Note that some of these reasons are easier to use as a basis for firing than others. For example, if you catch someone stealing from fellow employees, your course of action is clear: the employee will be fired, and there is not much reason to think deeply about it, except to make sure the evidence is airtight. Outright personality conflicts are also relatively easy, at least in extreme cases. The person must be either fired or transferred. Flagrant disobedience is also relatively easy, particularly where there is a consistent history of disobedience.

However, determining that someone does not have the skills to do a job, or in some other way does not measure up, is usually a difficult decision to make, except in the most extreme cases. Most such cases are not extreme; a person obviously lacking the requisite skills probably does not get a job in the first place. So, determining that a person's lack of skill is reason enough to fire him or her can be a long process—as can be the process of determining that an employee should be released for lack of motivation.

Reasons for Reluctance

Firing is an extreme use of your management authority. Your position in the organization which gives you the authority (at least theoretically) to fire someone is not based on natural law, or some God-given right. So, you may draw back from this most extreme use of the power you possess. That is only good sense, for the frequent use of extreme power blunts the effectiveness of that power.

There are also considerations of cost, to you, as an individual manager, and to your organization. When you fire someone, you create a vacancy that must be filled. This requires going through the often long and costly process of finding a replacement, and taking the risk that the replacement will not work out, either. While the position is being filled, your organization and your work unit will likely suffer.

A third consideration is your own reputation. If you end up firing a number of people, you will gain a reputation, not only among your subordinates, but among your superiors, too, as someone who fires a lot of people. What does that mean? Ultimately, it means you have failed as a manager of people, either to find the right people, or to manage them properly. It can come down to a difficult choice: fire someone to eliminate a problem in your organization, but at the same time risk building a reputation for yourself as someone who cannot handle people. An occasional firing will obviously not hurt you (it may even let people know you can make tough decisions), but frequent firings certainly can.

Often, too, a situation leading to termination is filled with emotions which affect everyone concerned. Actually firing someone will bring these emotions to the open and force them to be confronted in some way. That may be painful for all concerned.

Nonetheless, as a manager, you need always to face squarely the notion that firing someone is a distinct possibility. In some situations, it may be precisely the right decision.

Four Steps

Making the ultimate decision to dismiss someone should actually be reached in four distinct steps:

Step One: As said earlier, the first step is to decide that firing someone is a distinct possibility. You should come to this realization long before it can ever become a reality. The worst possibility is to let a problem develop to the point that there is finally a scene over some incident, during which you and the employee blow up, and the employee is told to leave suddenly. As a general rule, firing someone is something you should think about early and decide to do late. It is a last, but real, resort.

Step Two: Define the specific conditions under which you feel you must actually release the employee. Define here two points: 1) those conditions (a certain level of performance by the employee, for example) under which you will tell the employee that his job is in jeopardy, and 2) the level of performance at which you will actually and finally fire the employee.

Step Three: Warn the employee, as soon as conditions reach the point at which you had previously decided the employee should be warned. In a private interview, tell him that he is in danger of losing his job, explain precisely why he is in jeopardy, and describe what he must do to salvage his job. Explain all this clearly, and summarize it in writing.

Step Four: This, of course, is the period following the warning. The employee either improves or not. You should give the employee every reasonable chance and, in fact, give him or her as much help as possible to succeed. If he improves, tell him so. If he does not, and his performance reaches the point where you had decided he had to be fired, then you must do as you planned.

Keeping People Informed

So far in this discussion, the process has involved only you and the employee in question. As soon as you decide that an employee may deserve to be fired, you should tell the other key people involved—principally, your own boss. Depending on how your company is organized, you may want to inform other key people, too (with your boss's knowledge). The point here is not only to inform your boss and any others, but also to make them participants in the decision-making process. The overall principle here is the same as the one involved with the employee himself—the process should be confidential, but also as open as possible for those directly involved. No one, if and when anything happens, should be surprised.

Be candid with your boss about the reasons you are thinking of firing the employee. You might also want to review with your boss the plan you have developed for the problem, i.e., the conditions under which you will formally warn, and ultimately release, the employee.

The Final Step

Suppose you have followed the steps above and they have not worked; the employee has failed to improve, for whatever reason. You must now go ahead with the termination. Inform your own boss, and anyone else you brought into the matter, what is about to happen. Then, set up an actual meeting with the employee, at which you will tell him that he must leave.

Think through beforehand the specifics of the termination. There should be a specific leaving date—in most cases, it should be immediate (though pay will probably not stop immediately). Negotiate the public announcement, the reason given for the employee's leaving. If you wish, and if it is appropriate, give the employee the option of resigning. Under the process outlined in this chapter, many employees will have resigned by this point, anyway.

When you meet with the employee, tell him or her your decision and review the reasons for it. It should not be a surprise, though that does not mean it will be taken gracefully.

Review and settle with the employee those items (noted above) which you had thought through earlier. Then, lay out the employee's benefits and severance pay, if any. You might even explain what you are willing to say about him to those who will call you for references when he seeks another job.

It will depend on your judgment, but with some employees, it may be best to ask them to leave immediately, and you may even want to accompany them out. In an extreme case, this may be necessary to prevent the danger of the employee's taking records and information, or even committing vandalism.

Be sure to get from the employee any keys, passcards, identification cards, or any other company material that allows access to restricted areas.

Try to arrange an exit interview by another manager or someone from the personnel department. Because you are the one doing the firing, it would be best for you not to conduct this interview.

Finally, inform your boss about the results of the termination meeting. And be sure that key employees (not involved to this point) are informed of their fellow employee's leaving. They will probably hear it from the employee himself sooner or later. Be sure, in a pleasant way, that they understand your point of view.

Of course, if your company already has a procedure for terminations, you should find out through your boss and the personnel department what it is, and follow it.

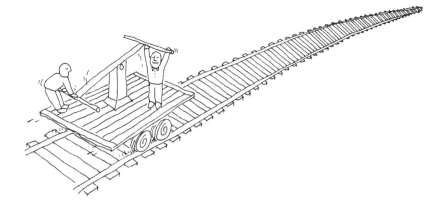

35 References and Further Reading

Much of this book is based on research I did over a two- or three-year period at one of the many business school libraries in Boston. I wrote the book in pieces—a necessary way to write when one is spending 50-plus hours a week at a full-time job. After choosing a topic (usually based on whatever management problem was then most prominent in my daily work), I did library research, mulled over the topic until I felt I understood it, and then wrote the chapter. Part III was written that way; when it was done, I wrote Parts I and II based on thoughts and ideas which arose from all the reading I had done for Part III. (Of course, it was not then called "Part III" because I did not know there would be Parts I and II.) My reading had led me to think about a number of issues in management—in fact, it led me to think about my own management activities—and those issues, combined with the conclusions I was reaching about my own work, eventually became Parts I and II after passing through countless drafts.

Thus, Part III is the portion of this book which owes the greatest direct debt to the writings of others. I want to acknowledge that debt in this chapter but, in doing so, I must be clear about the nature of that debt. I did not do research the way it normally is done, the way a student, for example, researches a term paper. I did not select a topic and then read everything there was to read on that topic. My goal was not to be scholarly and comprehensive. It was, instead, to clarify my own thinking about how I should approach a problem. When I felt I had read enough to understand the problem in my own mind, I stopped. On each topic, I probably missed some good sources of information. In addition, I must confess I approached each topic with a number of ideas of my own; usually, the research confirmed those ideas (which will confirm any cynics among you), and added sophistication and substance to them; sometimes, the research made me change my mind. The purpose, of the research, in short, was to help me grasp a problem, not to survey all that had been written on it.

My ultimate goal was not to present all relevant knowledge; indeed, it was in a sense the opposite—to present the minimum knowledge I thought was needed by a manager of people to do what managers do.

What follows then are only those sources on which I drew directly and obviously—studies or evidence referred to in the book, as well as those few instances where I consciously summarized someone else's ideas because I felt they were so valuable. There is no bibliography in the standard sense. It is not that I believe the ideas presented here are original with me; on the contrary. But, in most cases, I cannot trace them directly back to a single source.

The vast majority of references are for Part III, but Parts I and II require some brief commentary.

Parts I and II

As already mentioned, these portions of the book came indirectly out of the research done for Part III, which was written first. The Fundamental Cycle of Management is my own invention, though the ideas and concepts it embodies are certainly not new. They can be found expressed in a variety of ways in a large number of books on management. My hope is that the presentation of the ideas in the format of a cycle is helpful.

Many of the ideas in Part I concerning the manager-subordinate relationship came indirectly but clearly out of my reading on the subject of management control—how the manager makes sure the right things get done. Two articles deserve mention even though their influence was only seminal; you cannot blame them if you disagree with what I say in this book. They are:

A. S. Tannenbaum, "Control in organizations: Individual adjustment and organizational performance," *Administrative Science Quarterly*, vol. 7, 1962.

E. E. Lawler III, "Control systems in organizations," in *Handbook of Industrial and Organizational Psychology*," M. D. Dunnette, Ed. Chicago, IL: Rand-McNally College Publishing Co., 1976.

Part III

Chapter 12—"The Manager As Leader"
The research referred to can be found in: K. R. Student, "Supervisory influence and work-group performance," *Journal of Applied Psychology*, vol. LII, no. 3, 1968.

Chapter 13—"Helping Subordinates"
Many of the ideas here for how people learn came from: Leslie E. This and Gordon L. Lippitt, "Learning theories and training," *Training and Development Journal*, Apr./May, 1966. The model for learning in this chapter did not come from that article but from some long-ago source I cannot recall; its interpretation, however, is my own.

Chapter 15—"Managing Change Effectively"
The study referred to was reported in: D. A. Kolb, S. K. Winter, D. E. Berlew, "Self-directed change—two studies," *The Journal of Applied Behavioral Science*, vol. IV, no. 4, 1968.

Chapter 16—"Communicating As A Manager"
The data cited concerning openness in the manager-subordinate relationship can be found in: R. J. Burke and D. S. Wilcox, "Effects of different patterns and degrees of openness in superior-subordinate communication on subordinate job satisfaction," *Academy of Management Journal*, vol. XII, no. 3, 1969.

Chapter 17—"People and Decision-Making"
Much of the description of the problem-solving approach came from N. R. F. Maier and M. Sashkin, "Specific leadership behaviors that promote problem-solving," *Personnel Psychology*, vol. 24, 1971.

Chapters 21/22—"Work That Motivates" and "Steps for Enrichment"
A great deal has been written about job enrichment. The following articles provide valuable summaries: J. R. Hackman, G. Oldham, R. Janson, K. Purdy, "A new strategy for redesigning work," *California Management Review*, vol. XVII, no. 4, Summer, 1975.

The rest are from the *Harvard Business Review*:

R. N. Ford, "Job enrichment lessons from AT&T," Jan./Feb., 1973.
J. R. Hackman, "Is job enrichment just a fad?," May/June, 1973.
F. Herzberg, "One more time: How do you motivate employees?," Jan./Feb., 1968.

If you wish to pursue the notion of job-enrichment further, a good place to begin would be with J. R. Hackman, who has written extensively on the topic. Look him up in the card catalog of any good business library. Also, see my comments below about Frederick Herzberg.

Chapter 24—"Appraising Employees"
The work done at General Electric is described in H. H. Meyer, E. Kay, J. R. P. French Jr., "Split roles in performance appraisal," *Harvard Business Review*, Jan./Feb., 1965.

Chapter 28—"Money and Motivation"
The summary of Meyer's thoughts came from H. H. Meyer, "The pay-for-performance dilemma," *Organizational Dynamics*, Winter, 1975.

The study of pay satisfaction can be found in: K. Foster, J. Kanin-Lovers, J. Edwards, "Relationship of pay levels to pay satisfaction," from a report distributed by the American Compensation Association, Feb., 1976.

Chapter 30—"Managing Turnover"
This entire chapter is a summary of S. W. Gellerman's thoughts as presented in: "In praise of those who leave," *The Conference Board Record*, Mar., 1974.

Chapter 31—"Employees with Personal Problems"
Much of the material on alcoholism came from: J. W. Kelley, "Case of the alcoholic employee," *Harvard Business Review*, May/June, 1969.

The transposition of ideas in the chapter from alcoholism to employees' personal problems in general is entirely my own.

Chapter 33—"Salvaging the Marginal Employee"
This chapter owes a significant debt to: L. L. Steinmetz, "The unsatisfactory performer: Salvage or discharge," *Personnel*, May/June, 1968.

Chapter 34—"Firing an Employee"
The reference to "11%" came from: W. E. Scheer, *Personnel Administrators Handbook*, 2nd Edition, Chicago, IL: Dartnell, 1979, p. 180.

Further Reading

I have not personally found many books on management to be useful. You may have noticed that most of the above references come from periodicals. However, if you wish to read further about management in general, I can recommend various authors and books. Where specific books are mentioned, you might also want to look at other books or articles by the same authors.

I have not read everything by Peter Drucker, but I have been extremely impressed by what I have read. He writes clearly and sympathetically about management. Reading him will give you a strong sense of what management is and what managers do. I always recommend him to new managers, particularly his classics: *The Practice of Management* (1954) and *The Effective Executive* (1966). Both were published by Harper & Row in New York.

You may find the two other IEEE PRESS books on management to be useful. *General and Industrial Management*, by Henri Fayol, is a genuine classic by a real manager. Writing in 19th-century France, Fayol was the first to identify management's major components as planning, organizing, coordinating, commanding, and controlling. The IEEE PRESS edition was revised and updated in 1984 by Irwin Gray. The second book, *The Engineer in Transition to Management*, by Irwin Gray, deals specifically with the changes an engineer or other professional must make as he or she moves into management.

Frederick Herzberg writes about motivation (see reference above in Chapters 21/22) and presents various insights that I find intuitively right and even profound. In reviewing the literature on motivation, I sensed that other social scientists were not able to "prove" his assertions and, therefore, that he was slightly out of favor. But what he has to say about peoples' motivation will change the way you manage. His key book is *Work and the Nature of Man* (1966), published by T. Y. Crowell Co. in New York (distributed by Harper & Row, Scranton, PA). It's somewhat scholarly and certainly not light reading, and so I would recommend the article cited above (Chapters 21/22) as a nice summary.

L. R. Sayles has also co-authored two books (they appear to be textbooks) on the human side of management which present as nice an overview of managing people as any I have seen. They include *How Managers Motivate: The Imperatives of Supervision*, with W. F. Dowling, second edition, New York, NY: McGraw-Hill, 1978; and *Personnel: The Human Problems of Management*, with G. Strauss, fourth edition, Englewood Cliffs, NJ: Prentice-Hall, 1980.

Index

This is a topical index. Rather than listing every reference to various words, it tells you instead the location of major comments upon key management topics. It was compiled on the assumption that you will also look at the Table of Contents; thus it does not necessarily repeat all the information you can find there.

About the Author

L. Kent Lineback is Vice President and General Manager for New England Business Service, Inc. He manages a division which sells business products to businesses across the country. He also serves as a Director of a small company developing computer products.

Mr. Lineback previously served as Director of Marketing for Warren, Gorham & Lamont, a Boston publisher of professional books for lawyers, bankers, accountants, and tax practitioners. He was also Director of Administration for the Public Broadcasting Service and Director of Planning and Management Information for the Corporation for Public Broadcasting, both in Washington, DC. Early in his career, he spent several years as a consultant with the Sterling Institute in management education, working with such companies as CBS, DuPont, Metropolitan Life, GTE, and Peat, Marwick & Mitchell.

Mr. Lineback has a BA from Harvard and an MBA from Boston College. He is married, has three children and now lives near Boston.

OTHER IEEE PRESS BOOKS